Bring Me MY Chariot of Fire

Hugh C Shields

Grosvenor House
Publishing Limited

All rights reserved
Copyright © Hugh C Shields, 2017

The right of Hugh C Shields to be identified as the author of this work has been asserted in accordance with Section 78 of the Copyright, Designs and Patents Act 1988

The book cover picture is copyright to Hugh C Shields

This book is published by
Grosvenor House Publishing Ltd
Link House
140 The Broadway, Tolworth, Surrey, KT6 7HT.
www.grosvenorhousepublishing.co.uk

This book is sold subject to the conditions that it shall not, by way of trade or otherwise, be lent, resold, hired out or otherwise circulated without the author's or publisher's prior consent in any form of binding or cover other than that in which it is published and without a similar condition including this condition being imposed on the subsequent purchaser.

A CIP record for this book
is available from the British Library

ISBN 978-1-78623-842-9

Contents

Foreword by Allan Wells

Author's Note

Living Legend   1

    Chapter 1   The Last Survivor   3

Olympic Preparations   11

    Chapter 2   The First Encounter   13
    Chapter 3   The Man from No 84   20
    Chapter 4   I Shall Not Run On Sunday   26
    Chapter 5   Destination Paris   30

The Olympics   37

    Chapter 6   The Games Commence   39
    Chapter 7   The 100 Yards Final   43
    Chapter 8   The Second Encounter   50
    Chapter 9   The 400 Metres Final   55

Beyond the Olympics   61

    Chapter 10   Homecoming: Harold   63
    Chapter 11   Homecoming: Eric   68
    Chapter 12   The Elder Statesman of UK Athletics   75
    Chapter 13   The Legend of the Flying Scotsman   91

Postscript   107

    Chapter 14   Cambridge Revisited   109

Appendices

I	Career highlights – Harold Abrahams
II	Career highlights – Eric Liddell
III	Selected writings of Harold Abrahams
IV	Selected writings of Eric Liddell
V	Notes on the film Chariots of Fire
VI	Recollections of Eric Liddell by Sir Arthur Marshall
VII	Sir Arthur Marshall's Obituary in The Daily Telegraph
VIII	Notes on the title of the book
IX	Correspondence with Brian Boulton, former pupil of Eltham College
X	Article from The Daily Telegraph on unveiling of Liddell statue

Foreword by Allan Wells
1980 Olympic 100 metres champion

Firstly it is an enormous privilege to write a foreword for Bring Me My Chariot of Fire. I have been an enthusiastic admirer of Eric Liddell and Harold Abrahams for countless years, not only because they were immortalised in the outstanding film Chariots of Fire, but because of their diverse personalities and their motivation and dedication to achieve the ultimate athletic goal of winning an Olympic gold medal.

I had met Harold Abrahams in 1977 and although at that time he presented me with a medal for winning the British 60m indoor I didn't fully appreciate his achievements and what this meant to the English people. It was only after winning the 100m in Moscow in 1980, and in the press conference that followed, I was asked this question by an English reporter – "you did it for Harold Abrahams Allan didn't you!" After a few seconds and as a passionate Scot, I said "no, if I did it for anyone, I did it for Eric Liddell." I had known of Eric's epic story for many years, it was legendary, inspirational. I have great respect for him as an athlete and as a person.

If I were asked that same question today I would have to say "I did it for both." The change of sentiment is due to the emotion and the inspiration through films and books that these two legendary athletes have been described.

For anyone that has an interest in Eric Liddell and Harold Abrahams this book is a significant read! Essentially it informs you of the finest details in a book. It contains facts and figures of their performances before during and after the Olympics. It also tells of areas and experiences in their lives that convey a detailed account as people on and off the track. It provides an accurate description of events as they approach the 1924 Olympic games, and respectively follows their lives after their athletic careers, giving detail and information otherwise forgotten. It also catches the period of the sport when sporting honour meant so much.

Without doubt Hugh Shields has a passionate respect and a huge personal interest towards these two great athletes; he has been meticulous in capturing the written detail in their stories. I thank him for that, as it has been a pleasure to read and has made my understanding of two of Britain's greatest athletes significantly richer for the read.

Author's Note

This book tells the story of two of Great Britain's finest Olympic athletes, Eric Liddell and Harold Abrahams. Their achievements at the 1924 Paris Olympics, immortalised in the Oscar-winning film Chariots of Fire, are the stuff of legend. Like many films, Chariots of Fire contains elements of dramatic licence. In writing this book, I have sought to tell the true story to the extent that it is possible to glean it after all these years.

I want to place on record straight away that I think the film is magnificent. It beautifully evokes the two main characters and captures their respective entourages, including the great coach Sam Mussabini, with great charm. It is small wonder that the film won four Oscars, including Best Picture and Best Screenplay, despite its small budget. David Puttnam, Hugh Hudson and the late Colin Welland – who were respectively the Producer, Director and Screenplay Writer – made an absolute gem of a film.

I have long wanted to write this book. As a lifelong and passionate fan of athletics, this story has obvious and strong appeal. But the story also resonates for more personal reasons.

I am a Scot and Eric Liddell has been a hero since the time I first learned about him one morning in chapel at Trinity College Glenalmond[1] in Perthshire, where I went to school. My memory is a little hazy on the exact timing, but it definitely preceded

---

[1] The school is now simply known as Glenalmond College. But in my day, its religious foundation was explicitly reflected in its name.

Chariots of Fire which was released in 1981. That morning, one of the school's teachers spent ten minutes introducing us to this most remarkable of men. The school chapel was a fitting place to learn about Eric Liddell for the first time. For first and foremost, Eric was a Christian and a man who lived his life through God. Philippians 4:13 contains the oft-quoted words "I am able to do all things through Him who strengthens me." Those words are a powerful way to describe the way Liddell led his life. It is impossible to write about him, still less understand him, without an appreciation of his deep religious conviction which he sought by example to bring to others.

Other than being a great athlete, Eric was also an international rugby player. He appeared seven times for Scotland in the 1921 – 22 and 1922 – 23 seasons. Eric was one of two wingers – traditionally the fastest men on the pitch and often the try scorers. With his Christian beliefs, his athletic pedigree and his rugby prowess, Eric was (and still is) the perfect role model for a Scottish school such as the one I attended, where belief in the sport of rugby was nearly as important as belief in God! He was the original "muscular Christian", a ready hero for schoolchildren and adults alike.

Because of that Perthshire connection – as well as the fact that, for family reasons, I know Edinburgh and St Andrews – I know virtually every scene that was filmed in Scotland during the making of Chariots of Fire.

Another personal connection is that I attended the same Cambridge college, Gonville and Caius, as Harold Abrahams. I also won a Blue at Cambridge and captained the college athletics team some 60 odd years after Abrahams. As a Caian, I should at this point note that Chariots of Fire portrayed the college inaccurately and in a somewhat unflattering light in the film. If you have seen the film, you will recall that while at the college, Abrahams was depicted as someone who felt the weight of anti-semitic feeling most strongly. In reality, this was not the case – at least not to the extent made out in the film. Furthermore, it is not clear that the college frowned particularly on Abrahams' use of a coach. Eric Liddell also had a coach, a fact which is not apparent at all from the film. Today, the college is as proud of Harold Abrahams as any college could be.

Unlike my first book – Showdown in Moscow, which relates the rivalry of Seb Coe and Steve Ovett – I needed to do considerably more research for this book. My first thank you is to my father, Arthur Shields, who did some very interesting research in the annals of various Edinburgh libraries on Eric Liddell. The idea for Chapter 1 is also that of my father. The next thank you must go to Mark Ryan, whose meticulously-researched and detailed book on Harold Abrahams, Running with Fire, proved invaluable as a reference. I would also like to thank the Eric Liddell Centre in Edinburgh, whose records have been extremely helpful. I have, in addition, consulted a number of books about Eric Liddell. These were principally:

- John Keddie, Running the Race, Evangelical Press.
- David McCasland, Eric Liddell: Pure Gold: A New Biography Of The Olympic Champion Who Inspired Chariots Of Fire.
- Sally Magnusson. The Flying Scotsman.

I would like also to thank Allan Wells, for writing the wonderful foreword to this book. I would like to thank family friend and artist, Leigh Banks, who created the beautiful artwork that makes the cover of the book. And finally, I would like to thank Sue Pottle, the daughter of Harold Abrahams, for her encouragement and comments on the book.

I dedicate this book to my loving and supportive family, to the memory of Eric Liddell and Harold Abrahams and to everyone involved in the making of the cinematic masterpiece which is Chariots of Fire.

Hugh C Shields

January 2017

Living Legend

CHAPTER 1

The Last Survivor

"Hinc lucem et pocula sacra."
"From this place, we gain enlightenment and precious knowledge."
Official motto of the University of Cambridge.

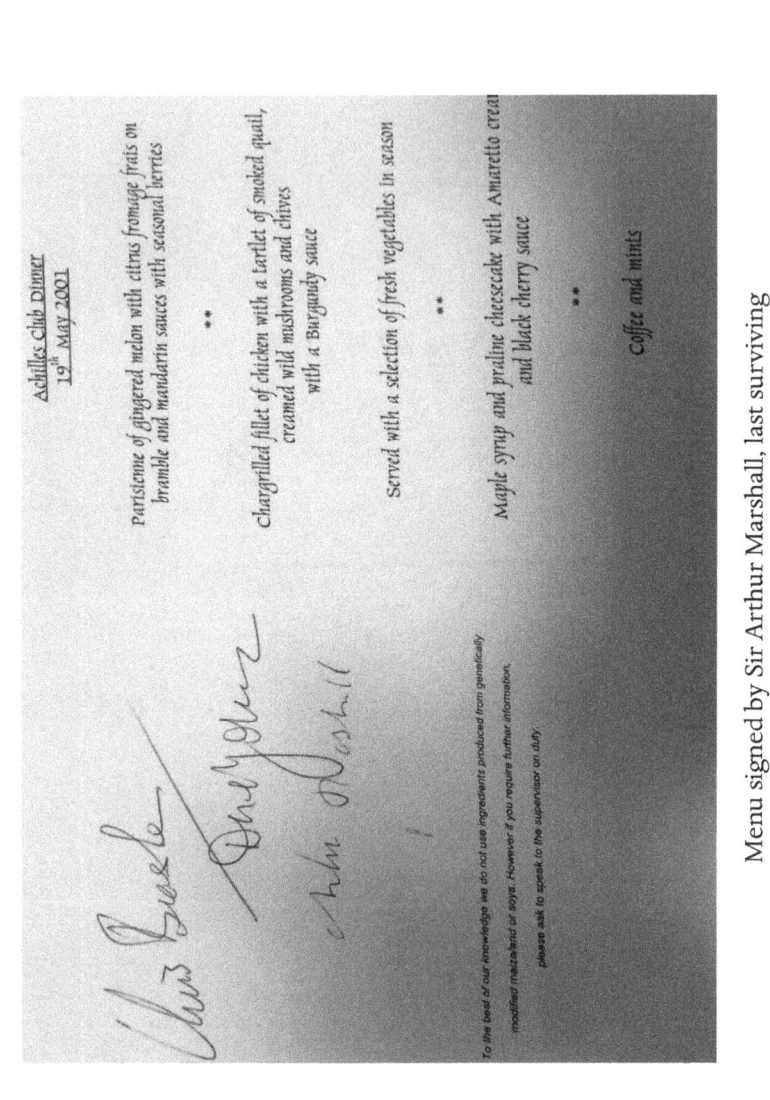

Achilles Club Dinner
19th May 2001

Parisienne of gingered melon with citrus fromage frais on bramble and mandarin sauces with seasonal berries

**

Chargrilled fillet of chicken with a tartlet of smoked quail, creamed wild mushrooms and chives with a Burgundy sauce

Served with a selection of fresh vegetables in season

**

Maple syrup and praline cheesecake with Amaretto cream and black cherry sauce

**

Coffee and mints

To the best of our knowledge we do not use ingredients produced from genetically modified maize/and or soya. However if you require further information, please ask to speak to the supervisor on duty.

Menu signed by Sir Arthur Marshall, last surviving member of the 1924 Olympic team

9pm, Saturday 19th May 2001
Robinson College dining room, Cambridge University

I cannot quite believe that I am talking to the last surviving member of the 1924 Great Britain Olympic team. I also know that this gentleman had more than a passing acquaintance with both Harold Abrahams and Eric Liddell. Sir Arthur Marshall, who travelled to the 1924 Paris Olympics as a reserve on the 440 yards relay squad, is now 96 years old and has had a distinguished career as an aviation engineer[2]. But he had also been a Blue at Cambridge with Harold Abrahams and had got to know Eric Liddell as well at the Olympics in 1924. Arthur Marshall in fact knew the real story so well that, when he saw Chariots of Fire for the first time, he said he "was horrified by the extent to which the facts had been distorted".

I am attending the dinner which follows the annual Varsity Athletics match between Oxford and Cambridge and which is organised by the Achilles Club. On this occasion, there seem to be athletic luminaries wherever you look. I am seated opposite Derek Johnson, 800 metres Silver medallist at the 1956 Melbourne Olympics. On the next table sits Chris Brasher, the 3000 metres steeplechase Gold medallist at those same Melbourne Games and – more famously – one of the pacers for Roger Bannister's four minute mile. But, with my unbridled interest in the film Chariots of Fire, I am truly captivated to meet Arthur Marshall.

---

[2] Sir Arthur Marshall died in 2007 at the age of 103 and, by kind permission of The Daily Telegraph, I have reproduced his obituary in Appendix III. You will see that he was a giant of a man in all senses.

10 am Saturday March 31, 1923
Hyde Park, London

Arthur Marshall and Harold Abrahams were both competing for Cambridge University in the 1923 Varsity match. For Harold, it was the fourth time he had done so and on this occasion, he was Captain of the team. This meant he had almost sole discretion as to who got selected for which event. It also brought pressure to deliver results and lead by example.

Harold was by this stage well established both as a 100 yards sprinter and long jumper. His track record in the Varsity match up to that point was enviable: he had already won the 100 yards three times and, if he could win a fourth time, he would make history by becoming the only undergraduate ever to have done so. He had also competed successfully at the long jump, having won the event twice before. As Captain of the team in his final year as an undergraduate, he was keen not only to make his mark but to do something truly memorable and go out on a real high. Much to the surprise of other members of the team, Harold decided to select himself not only for the 100 yards and long jump but also the 440 yards. This last decision was without question controversial: Harold had no history at the longer sprint event and his Oxford adversaries found the decision laughable. Oxford, meanwhile, were fielding W.E. ('Bill') Stevenson, an American with real star quality at the event. Stevenson had previously won the United States Amateur Championship, had broken 49 seconds for 440 yards and had never been beaten at the distance in England. As a Rhodes scholar, he was regarded as a mercurial talent by his Oxford team mates. Oxford could scarcely believe that Cambridge were going to put Abrahams up against him. Little did they know that they were about to learn something about the real Harold Abrahams that would surprise even the cynical.

The other Cambridge 440 yard runner was Arthur Marshall. Arthur Marshall had significant pedigree at the event and was certainly considered the 'A' string runner. Indeed, as the stronger runner, he might have expected to have been consulted on Harold's selection of himself. But this had not happened and now the day of reckoning had arrived.

On the morning of the Varsity match, Harold invited Arthur for a walk to the Peter Pan statue in Hyde Park. They were already in London because the match itself was taking place at the Queen's Club in West Kensington. Harold's opening question was simple: did Arthur think he could beat Bill Stevenson, the talented American from Oxford? Arthur candidly acknowledged that he didn't think he had a "dog's chance". Emboldened with this knowledge, Harold explained his plan. He, Harold, would sprint to the front of the field at the start of the race when the runners broke from their lanes. He would then slow the race down and lure the Oxford runners into a false a sense of security, with Arthur also falling in line with the artificially slow pace. Then, in the finishing straight, Harold would attempt to unlock a finishing burst to take victory for himself. If he was horrified by the cunning of it, Arthur did not show it. Out of loyalty to the team, he had no choice but to go with the plan. And so they made their way to the Queens' Club with an audacious scheme to defeat the great Bill Stevenson.

12 am, Saturday March 31, 1923
The Queen's Club, West Kensington, London

Harold was by now in a good state of mind to make the day his own. But the build-up to the event had been fraught. For one thing, the Cambridge team had been plagued by injuries and drop-outs. But Harold himself had suffered a severe bout of nerves just the day before. He was carrying a minor foot injury and this was playing on his mind. Furthermore, he had woken up with a sore throat, become feverish and decided on a visit to his older brother Adolphe, a doctor. After examining him thoroughly, Adolphe pronounced him fit and well and told him it was all in the mind. Buoyed up by his brother's decisive assessment, Harold's confidence returned.

For Harold, the first event of the day was the most glamorous of all, the 100 yards. Conditions were good and Harold raced into an immediate three yard lead which he maintained comfortably. Harold sped through the line in 10.0 seconds to take an easy victory. This was the wonderful start Harold had been seeking, for it sealed his place in history as the only undergraduate to have won the short sprint four times in a row.

Barely twenty minutes later, Harold was in action again in the long jump. Would his injured foot hold up? Harold was banking on a single big jump – partly to protect his weak foot but partly also because he need to conserve energy for the 440 yards. Harold's first jump was big but, alas, a "no jump" since he was several inches beyond the take-off board. Harold needed to nail his second jump in order to protect his chances in the longer sprint event. Amassing all the concentration he could, he sped down the runway and put in a massive effort. This time Harold was safely behind the board and he leapt to a new Varsity record distance of 23 feet 7 inches and a quarter. Harold could retire from the long jump competition knowing that his performance would not be bettered.

It was now time for Harold's final individual event, the 440 yards, and the showdown with Bill Stevenson. As pre-agreed, Harold set off at a furious pace and immediately took the lead. Exactly as planned, he then slowed the pace down and settled into the race. Both Oxford runners fell in behind Arthur Marshall, who they regarded as the real threat. Harold continued at this steady pace until they rounded the bend into the final straight, at which point he moved aside in an apparent gesture to let Arthur Marshall through. But Arthur Marshall made no move and Bill Stevenson, believing now that he simply had to overtake Marshall to win, similarly made no move. The ruse had worked. Moments later, Harold exploded into life and made a decisive move for the finishing line. Pouring every ounce of effort into the final part of the race, Harold crossed the line in 50.8 seconds, around a second faster than he had ever run the distance before. The crowd were ecstatic, giving Harold a standing ovation. Fulsome reports of Harold's exploits appeared in the press and, despite the fact that Cambridge had lost the team event to Oxford, the day very much belonged to the Cambridge captain.

Harold had completed his university athletics career on a high, in no small part due to the support of Arthur Marshall. But was Harold truly the best in the land? In the summer of 1923, Harold was about to be confronted with a Scottish athlete of remarkable talent who would test the limits of both his physical and mental capabilities.

Olympic Preparations

CHAPTER 2

The First Encounter

"On his way to the top, a runner must have ambition together with iron will. Money does not make a runner, but a deep desire from within."
Paavo Nurmi in 1971

Stamford Bridge, London, 6 July 1923

Amateur Athletic Association ('AAA') Championships

The starter's pistol fired and Eric Liddell launched himself down the track with total commitment. Although an ungainly runner, the Scot's determination and will to win were already legendary. And on this day, Eric's determination was as great as ever. For alongside him ran Harold Abrahams, the Olympic hopeful from Cambridge University. This was the semi-final of the 220 yards sprint at the 1923 AAA championships and the first time the two had raced each other.

The Rise of the Flying Scotsman

By 1923, Eric had firmly established himself among the international sprinting elite. His rise had been meteoric. Only two years earlier, in February 1921 and aged 19, he had started at Edinburgh University as a highly promising schoolboy sprinter. But between May and August of that year, Eric produced a sequence of races which brought him immediate international success.

Eric began at the Craiglockhart ground by winning the Edinburgh University Athletics Club 100 yards title, defeating the more experienced and favoured G Innes Stewart in a time of 10.4 seconds. He also took second in the 220 yards. Having earned selection for the Edinburgh University Team, Eric then proceeded to win both the 100 and 220 yards titles at the Scottish intervarsity championships in St Andrews. A week later, Eric took both sprint titles at the Scottish Amateur Athletic Association's Championships in Glasgow. And on July 9, at a triangular international in Belfast, Eric won the 100 yards.

Eric's achievements had not gone unnoticed. On August 11 1921, the Glasgow Herald reported that "His success has been phenomenal; in fact it is one of the romances of the amateur path. Unknown four months ago, he today stands at the forefront of British sprinters.....Liddell, as much because of his supreme grit as because of his pace, is a great figure in modern athletics, and is destined to be still greater in the future."

It was all a far cry from Tientsin (Tianjin) in North China, where Eric was born the second son of the Reverend and Mrs James Dunlop Liddell in 1902. The Liddells were Scottish missionaries with the London Missionary Society and Eric was schooled in China until the age of five. At the age of six, he and his elder brother Rob were sent to Eltham College in Blackheath, London, a boarding school for the sons of missionaries. Their parents and sister Jenny returned to China, returning home only infrequently for extended stays known as "furloughs". During the boys' time at Eltham their parents, sister and new brother Ernest came home on furlough just two or three times during the entire time the boys were there. On these occasions, they got together as a family in Scotland, often in Edinburgh. It was a family lifestyle of unbelievable austerity and a reflection of the Liddells' true missionary zeal.

At Eltham, Eric quickly set himself apart as an outstanding sportsman. He was awarded the Blackheath Cup as the best athlete of his year in 1918 and became Captain of both the cricket and rugby teams. Eric also set the school record for 100 yards at 10.2 seconds and there is evidence that this record was never broken before the school switched to metric measures. As outlined in Appendix IX, Brian Boulton describes how there apparently was a wind-assisted time faster than Eric's 10.2 benchmark. But, correctly, Brian would not validate the time owing to the favourable wind conditions. So Eric's time, set in

1919, was never surpassed. Despite his sporting heroics, Eric's headmaster described him as being "entirely without vanity". To this day, one of the boarding houses at Eltham College is named Liddell House in Eric's honour.

On finishing Eltham, Eric went in the Autumn of 1919 to Edinburgh University where his elder brother Rob was already studying. Although he took his studies seriously, Eric also pursued his aptitude for sport with passion. From the outset, he played rugby for the university and his devastating speed and fearless approach brought him quickly to the top of the sport: in 1922 Eric was selected to play for Scotland. In the 1922 and 1923 seasons, Eric played for Scotland a total of seven times. Eric put heart and soul into every game and, although not always as consistent as he might have liked, he was a consummate player at his very best.

With the Paris Olympics beckoning in 1924, Eric realised that he would benefit from focusing solely on athletics in the run-up to the games. By the time the AAA championships came round in July 1923, Eric had already made that commitment and would never play rugby for Scotland again. Feeling God's calling to athletics, he decided to pour all his sporting energies into that. His faith gave him a strength and confidence in competition that Harold could only envy. For athletics at the highest level is not just a matter of physical prowess. The self-belief has to be there too. And Eric had it in spades, fuelled as he was by the conviction that he was running God's race every time he stepped on the track. The contrast with Harold could not have been greater.

The Cambridge Blue

Harold Abrahams was born to Jewish parents in December 1899 and was one of six children. His father, Isaac Coniums, came from what is now Lithuania but which at the time was known as

Russo-Poland. His mother Esther Isaacs, was of Polish descent. Isaac took the name Abrahams from his father Abraham Coniums. Despite barely being able to speak a word of English on his arrival in England, Isaac applied himself assiduously to making money. Starting from modest beginnings, he built up a successful career in money lending and became wealthy enough to send Harold to a succession of good schools. The last of these, Repton, gave Harold enough of a springboard to get into Cambridge University – although it seems that his father's wealth may also have played a part. Harold excelled on the athletics track although did not particularly distinguish himself in the classroom. In any event, he did enough to gain entry to Gonville and Caius College, one of Cambridge University's older colleges, to read Law.

Harold enjoyed immediate athletic success at Cambridge, gaining his coveted "Blue" in his first year as an undergraduate. In order to win a Blue, you have to compete for either Oxford or Cambridge in the annual Varsity match between the two. It is a prestigious achievement and Harold was proud to have secured it so quickly. In the 1920s, Oxford and Cambridge supplied many of Great Britain's international athletes and it was a fertile hunting ground for Olympic selectors. Harold himself competed in the 1920 Antwerp Olympics and, whilst he did not take any medals, it would provide valuable experience four years later. By 1923, his final undergraduate year, Harold had laid the foundation for some strong Olympic performances. But there was still much to be done.

Stamford Bridge, London, 23 July 1923

AAA Championships

Eric Liddell stormed through the 220 yards semi-final as if his life depended on it. In doing so, he left Harold Abrahams floundering in his wake. The race was not even close: Eric crossed the line in 21.6 seconds, some four yards ahead of Harold. In fact, Harold did not even finish a clear second: another athlete, William Nichol, stopped the clock at 22.0 seconds, exactly the same time as Harold. The two athletes were declared to be in equal second place. If Harold wanted to make the final, he would need to do a run-off against Nichol. It was looking a tall order for Harold actually to win the event outright at this point.

Harold once more seemed to be fighting his mental demons for he announced his withdrawal from the championships not long after his defeat. Citing a sore throat, he gave up the possibility of a place in the 220 yards final as well as the blue riband event, the 100 yards. And, as if to add insult to injury, Eric Liddell not only won the 220 yards the following day but scorched to a blistering 9.7 seconds victory in the 100 yards as well. This time was a British record and would stand for fully 35 years. It was a time well beyond Harold's best at the time and even years later, Harold cast doubt upon its veracity. But Eric had found a purple patch of form and the conditions – warm and still – were about as perfect as could be found in London.

Harold had been decisively and convincingly outclassed by Eric. Harold had not been in the right place mentally and, for all his heroic performances at the Varsity match just months earlier, his Olympic ambitions would founder if he could not find some additional ingredient. Fortunately Harold's luck was about to change in the most helpful of ways. He was about to link up with the most advanced athletics coach of his generation, a man whose influence is felt even today in 21st century athletics. This was a man who inspired multiple athletes in different sports and disciplines to Olympic and national titles. This was a master coach who left no stone unturned in his quest for the ultimate performance. This was a man who was about to cast his magic spell upon Harold in a way that Harold could not even imagine.

CHAPTER 3

The Man from No 84

"The ability to prepare is more important than the ability to compete. It is not about the race. It is about the preparation."
Haile Gebreselassie

The blue plaque at No. 84 Burbage Road in
Herne Hill where Sam Mussabini lived
Photograph courtesy of Susan Irvine and John Benger.

Number 84, Burbage Road, Herne Hill, South London

June 2012

It is just a matter of days before the London 2012 Olympics begin. Gathered around the front of number 84 Burbage Road in Herne Hill is a small group of people who have come to honour a man known in his day simply as Sam. For a blue plaque is being unveiled to celebrate the remarkable achievements of Sam Mussabini. Sam lived on Burbage Road from 1913 until his death in 1927. In large part because of the sophistication and professionalism of his approach, Sam was not a welcome part of the British athletic establishment at the time. That establishment remained very much set in its amateur ways: the gifted gentleman amateur could not be seen to be overly dedicated or serious in approach. The blue plaque would, in a small way, redress the balance and ensure Sam secured the respect and appreciation he always deserved as a coach.

Sam Mussabini was born in London in 1867 to a family of mixed Syrian, Turkish, French and Italian origins. By the time he died, Sam could fairly lay claim to being one of the finest coaches this country has ever seen. His full name at birth was Scipio Arnaud Godolphin Mussabini but he decided at some point to replace his middle two names with the name Africanus. So it was that Scipio Africanus Mussabini took the first letters of each of his names and became simply Sam. And it was to Sam that Harold Abrahams turned in 1923 in order to supercharge his Olympic efforts.

Sam had wide-ranging interests in many sports. He was an accomplished billiards player, acted as a referee and also wrote widely about the game. In 1904, he published a two volume work on the detailed technicalities of the sport. These books, containing many hundreds of drawings, illustrate graphically Sam's fanatical attention to detail. He had a strong interest in cricket but the two sports in which he dedicated most time as a coach were athletics and cycling. His house on Burbage Road in fact backed on to the Herne Hill velodrome and was the perfect base for his cycle coaching.

By the time Harold Abrahams linked up with him in 1923, Sam had already enjoyed considerable success with Olympic athletes. The 1908 Olympics had taken place in London and Sam had worked with the South African sprinter Reggie Walker to improve his technique and starting speed. Walker took gold and became the first of Sam's athletes to win Olympic medals. The most successful of Sam's athletes was Albert Hill, who took gold in both the 800 and 1500 metres in the 1920 Olympics. This was a feat which was not repeated by a British athlete until Dame Kelly Holmes took the Sydney Olympics by storm and did the same double. In all, Sam's athletes won a total of eleven Olympic medals.

Sam began working with sprinters at the Polytechnic Harriers Club in 1894 and thus had nearly 30 years of athletic coaching experience behind him by the time he took on Harold. He had even, in the early 1920s, begun to experiment with cinematography and had acquired a tripod and camera so that he could film and then analyse in detail the style and techniques of his athletes. Harold was a significant beneficiary of this new technology, as they filmed and then pored over detailed sequences of Harold's sprinting style.

From Harold's point of view, Sam's detailed technical attention was exactly what he needed. It gave him much needed additional confidence, the confidence which comes from knowing that everything possible has been done to deliver the best result. They would spend hours working on this technique in the sports grounds of London, including Paddington Recreation Ground and Queen's Club in West Kensington. Sam analysed and sought to improve every part of Harold's race in his quest to extract those precious extra yards which could so easily mean the difference between victory and defeat. It was essential for Harold to get a good start: in the 100 yards, a poor start might prove irrecoverable. Thus they worked tirelessly on improving Harold's pick-up and drive to full sprint speed. Once up to full speed, which would be around 30 yards from the start, it was then essential to maintain form through to the finishing line. In this phase of the race, Sam placed great emphasis on smooth arm action. Sam appreciated more than most that running is a "whole body" sport – in order to get the legs to turn over as fast as possible, the whole body must be operating in unison. Finally, there was the push to the finishing line, where a judicious lunge just yards out would ensure that the chest came across the line as early as possible.

Harold poured his heart and soul into his training with Sam, knowing that every additional effort could help him succeed in his ultimate quest for gold at the Olympics. Harold was by now training far harder than any other contemporary – his 15 to 20 weekly training hours represented perhaps 10 times the training volume of some of his would-be competitors. Professional in approach if not professional in pure money terms, Harold's efforts set him apart as someone who was completely driven – someone so keen to win Olympic gold that he would stop at nothing to gain fair advantage. This advanced and committed training approach would undoubtedly pay dividends.

But Harold was also to be the beneficiary of another helpful development which was completely outside his control. After the 1923 AAA Championships, Harold was suddenly faced with serious competition from another British athlete. Whereas previously, he might have thought his competition was going to come from overseas – and especially the United States – he now had to face the prospect that he might not even be the top British sprinter. Eric Liddell was, however, about to make Harold's quest for gold a rather easier proposition.

CHAPTER 4

I Shall Not Run On Sunday

"They will mount up with wings like eagles. They will run and not be weary." Isaiah 31

On March 22 1924, the athletics schedule for the Paris Olympics was published. The schedule made clear that the 100 metres heats were to take place on a Sunday. Furthermore, the heats of both the 100 metres and 440 yards relays were also to take place on a Sunday.

For Eric the significance could not have been greater. The Sabbath was sacrosanct: he could not permit himself to compete on a Sunday. But Eric did not make an immediate fuss. For one thing, he had received a special invitation to join a small band of Oxford and Cambridge athletes to compete in the Penn relays in the United States on April 25th and 26th. These relays, hosted by the University of Pennsylvania, still take place to this day and remain a high profile meeting at which athletes can test their early season abilities against some of their strongest peers. Eric's invitation included an entry to the 100 metres. The local competition would be fierce and the American sprinters would rightly regard the "flying Scot", as he was now known, as an Olympic contender. The 100 metres would without doubt be one of the highlights of the meeting. It just seemed inappropriate to spell out at this early stage that he would not be doing the 100 metres at the Games themselves. Furthermore, there were still some weeks to go before Olympic selections were finalised. It might seem presumptuous to declare his position immediately.

The invited athletes set sail for the United States in April 1924. Eric was laid low by severe sea sickness – hardly an auspicious start. On arrival, Eric was able to recover his strength relatively quickly while staying at the Pennsylvania Cricket Club. This was fortunate, for the 100 metres was quickly upon him. In the event, Eric could only finish fourth in a close-run race won by Chester Bowman of Syracuse University in 10.0 seconds. Eric had run

10.1 seconds but had been beaten by three other athletes. Eric fared better in the 220 yards, where he placed second to Louis Clark of John Hopkins University. But the sobering reality was that Eric had been soundly beaten and the best American sprinters – Charlie Paddock and Jackson Scholz – were not even there. If Eric needed any further encouragement to withdraw from the Olympic 100 metres on account of the Sabbath, this was surely it.

Among those who had been invited to the Penn relays was Arthur Marshall and he and Eric quickly struck up a friendship on the return voyage. Eric's humility and sense of fun were much more to Arthur's liking than the more highly strung and self-absorbed Harold. There was, indeed, fun to be had and they both joined in the spirit of things, including the fancy dress dance. They spent time with two American ladies, playing Mah Jong and cards. They spoke about the forthcoming Olympics and even promised to catch up with the two young ladies in Paris once the games were over.

With the Penn relays behind him, Eric declared his position. Since Eric was considered the number one British 100 metres runner, this news did not play well with the British Olympic Committee. The Committee called Eric in to explain himself. To members of the Committee, the notion that an individual athlete could defy their wishes seemed almost heretical – surely, it seemed to them, their decision to select an athlete was an honour which every athlete should regard as such. It never occurred to them – and certainly had not happened before – that an athlete might simply reject their decision. He patiently explained his position to the Committee as well as several other grandees of the British athletic establishment. Eric's position was absolutely clear and absolutely immovable. To Eric, no amount of debate or influencing would ever cause him to change his mind. There was not even a "decision" to be discussed: his position on the Sabbath was resolute.

From Harold's point of view, his Olympic challenge was made at once easier. He could now focus on his overseas challengers safe in the knowledge that he would not be outdone by someone from his own shores. Psychologically, it was a significant boost to Harold for he could be confident in his own mind that, whatever else, he was the British number one. There is no question that Harold felt the better for it. Harold had been psychologically crushed by Eric at the 1923 AAA Championships: the firm knowledge that this experience could not be repeated at the Olympics was a real bonus as he made his final preparations for the games.

But what of Eric? What was his strategy to be now that the short sprint was not on the agenda? There was always the option of the longer sprint, the 220 yards. Eric did not discount competing at that distance and indeed remained very much open to the possibility. But he decided to focus most of his efforts and energies on the 440 yards. Perhaps the sprinting talent on display at the Penn relays caused him to doubt be could get the ultimate prize at the 220 yards. Or perhaps he realised he had untapped talent at the longer distance. Either way, the 440 yards was the principal race now in Eric's sights. Eric had little track record at the distance and time was short. Could he make the race his own? The waiting world would not have to ponder too long to find out.

CHAPTER 5

Destination Paris

"Citius, Altius, Fortius."
The Olympic motto, which is Latin for "Faster, Higher, Stronger." The motto was proposed by Pierre de Coubertin on the creation of the International Olympic Committee in 1894.

By May 1924, Eric had begun to focus in earnest on the 440 yards. In that month he ran two races over the distance, completing each in a little over 51 seconds. Such a time was not going to set the world alight. But it was a start and made clear his intentions.

Meanwhile Harold continued to battle his inner demons, despite being far fitter and better prepared than any of his contemporaries. The fact that he had publicly prepared so much more assiduously than anyone else set him up for ignominious failure should he not win. This thought preyed heavily on Harold's mind every time he competed. The contrast with Eric could not have been greater. Eric ran in God's name and with God's will. There was nothing to worry about for the outcome was always simply of God's making. Should he not win, this was God's wish and there would be another race on another day. But for Harold – and despite his Jewish religious upbringing – racing was a much more intense and personal affair. Once on the start line, Harold alone carried the burden of success or failure. And Harold alone enjoyed the fruits of victory or carried the pains of defeat.

Despite internalising all his worries, Harold managed to notch up several high class performances in the run up to the Olympics. In a series of competitions during May 1924 – including the Middlesex Championships, the Midland Counties Championships and the Achilles versus Services match – Harold took multiple victories in both the 100 yards and the long jump. But he reserved one of his finest efforts for a match on 7 June at Woolwich. Harold was timed at 9.6 seconds for the 100 yards, a time which then equalled the world record. There was a slight following wind and Harold himself doubted whether it intrinsically matched the fastest time ever recorded. Harold – who was often very honest with himself about his own performances – thought no more about it and certainly made no attempt to have the time ratified. By contrast, his long jump that day – measured at 24 feet 2 1/2 inches (equivalent to 7.38 metres) – established an English record which was to stand for 30 years.

Harold's intensive training protocols drew mixed responses. Many of his fellow Oxbridge athletes continued to play the part of the "gentleman amateur": the notion that one might deliberately pour hours and hours into training was considered by most to be "de rigeur". Harold knew this was often the reaction but remained absolutely committed to his approach. In many ways, Harold's work with Sam Mussabini was the first real forerunner of modern day elite training programmes. Today it is a given that, in order to reach the top of athletics, full time commitment is needed. Sprint drills, video analysis and daily contact with a coach are also commonplace.

However it was regarded, Harold's collaboration with Sam was really beginning to pay dividends and he was very much seen as Great Britain's leading athlete. But Eric was also training hard and continued to work closely with his coach Tom McKerchar. Eric's build-up to the Olympics, although less high profile than Harold's, was not short of impressive performances. Notable among these was his series of wins at Hampden park on June 14 at the Scottish Championships. Eric took the 100 yards in 10.0 seconds, the 220 yards in 21.6 seconds and the 440 yards in 51.2 seconds. Although he had withdrawn from the Olympic 100 metres, this did not stop him using the shorter sprint event for speed training – and it perhaps gave some indication of how he ultimately planned to race the 440 yards when it came to the Olympics itself.

The last significant domestic competition before the Olympics was the AAA Championships at Stamford Bridge in London.

Harold was entered for both the 100 yards and the long jump and, as in his earlier competitions that year, he felt the pressure to deliver to an acute degree – even though Eric was not running in the 100 yards. In the event, Harold easily defeated the 100 yards field, running 9.9 seconds in the process. Although rather slower than Eric's 9.6 seconds from the year before, Harold delighted the crowd by the ease of his victory. But he fell short of his highest standards in the long jump, where he managed 22 feet 6 1/2 inches (equivalent to 6.87 metres). Press comment was mixed but at least Harold had come through in the blue riband event.

Eric, meanwhile put in a big effort over 440 yards, winning the race in 49.6 seconds. This time was still not competitive with the best in the world. But it was faster than his previous month's races and he was building to a peak in Paris. Eric also finished second in the 220 yards, completing the race in 21.7 seconds just behind the South African Howard Kinsman. Overall, Eric was satisfied with his performances. They laid a solid foundation for the cauldron of Olympic competition to come – and indeed his performances that weekend confirmed his selection at both distances.

All was now set fair for Paris. The Great Britain team comprised some 70 athletes – which was far too many in Harold's opinion. Writing in the Daily Express on June 25 under the heading "By a famous international athlete", Harold made his position abundantly clear:

"The team is much larger than that sent to Antwerp four years ago, and it is to be hoped that the British Olympic Association have sufficient funds at their disposal to justify the inclusion of a good many athletes who must of necessity, from the point of view of Olympic achievement, be ranked as 'also rans'."

This was not the first time Harold had written critically of his fellow athletes – he had written a similar article earlier in April and had made no attempt to disguise his identity. So his fellow athletes would make the connection with Harold in his latest piece. It was typical of Harold to write such words and, knowing perfectly well that they would cause resentment among the team, publish anyway. Harold was never one to court publicity for its own sake. Brutal honesty was – at least when it suited him – more his stock in trade.

Harold had not just written about his fellow athletes. He had even written about himself in a bid to have himself deselected from the Olympic long jump competition:

"H.M. Abrahams is chosen for four events, which is unfortunate. From the point of view of the Olympic Games, this athlete should leave the long jump severely alone. The authorities surely do not imagine that he can perform at long jumping at two o'clock and running 200 metres at 2.30 on the same afternoon. Let us hope that Abrahams has been told by the authorities to concentrate his efforts on the 100 metres."

Remarkably, the British Olympic Association did indeed offer Harold the opportunity to withdraw from the long jump. Harold readily accepted the offer and could now focus his attention exclusively on his sprinting.

Harold and Eric were now both ready for Paris. Harold was entered in the events he wanted – the 100 metres, the 200 meters and the sprint relay – and he had done everything possible to prepare. He even felt the weight of Olympic competition rather less compared to his domestic appearances: the might of the

American athletes meant that Harold could not be regarded as an obvious favourite for either the 100 metres or the 200 metres. Rather, he was in the position of being able to give the races his all and having nothing to lose. Eric, meanwhile, had sharpened up nicely for both the races he would take on – the 200 metres and the 440 yards. As ever, he did not feel the weight of competition. He would run in God's name and what would be would be.

The Olympics

CHAPTER 6

The Games Commence

"Those of us who had the good fortune to watch the spectacle will never again see anything to equal it in its splendour. Not even the most phlegmatic of us could fail to be thrilled at the sight of the wiliest and lithest bodies of the athletes of forty five nations, clad each in their respective national uniforms, and marching with heads erect behind their flagbearers."

Henry Stallard, GB representative in the 800 metres and 1500 metres at the 1924 Olympics and also a member of Gonville and Caius College.

Arriving in Paris at the Gare de Nord after their long and arduous sea crossing, the Great Britain team was met by a welcoming party of some standing. There was Earl Cadogan and General Kentish from the British Olympic Committee as well as several other leading dignitaries including the British Ambassador. After polite formalities, the team was escorted to the Hotel Moderne in the Place de la Republique. Although central, the hotel was modest: compared with the US, the Great Britain team was running to a tight budget and there were to be no excesses over and beyond the basics. The effects of the First World War were still being all too keenly felt.

At 10 am on Saturday July 5th, all athletes gathered at Notre Dame for a church service in their honour. It was a suitably majestic and serious note on which to start the day's proceedings. After the service, the athletes made their way to the Stade de Colombes in readiness for the opening ceremony. In time-honoured fashion, each team paraded through the stadium with their flag, saluting the President's box as they went. The largest team by far was that of the Americans who had come with some 350 athletes. In total there were over 3,000 competitors in Paris and 45 nations.

The US had brought four world-class sprinters in the shape of Charlie Paddock, Jackson Scholz, Chester Bowman and Lauren Murchison. Any one of these sprinters could claim the Olympic 100 metres title and each was hungry to do so. But did any of them have the mental desire to match that of Harold? To Harold, this race meant everything. His desire ran deeply into his very heart and soul.

There was one last preparatory step for Harold to follow. Carefully, he took a measured amount of a tonic called Easton's syrup. This tonic contained a small amount of strychnine and, in the right dosage, was an effective stimulant for a sprinter. Today, such a drug would be banned. But in the 1924 Olympics, there was no such ban on these drugs. This would help Harold negotiate multiple rounds of the 100 metres and 200 metres as well as the relay.

The opening round of the 100 metres took place on July 5. Harold ran in Heat 14 along with Carr of Australia. Although Harold comfortably qualified in 11.0 seconds, he was most dissatisfied with its performance and sought immediate guidance from Philip Noel-Baker. Noel-Baker advised Harold to warm up fully and in preparation for the second round of the 100 metres, this is exactly what Harold did.

This time Harold completed the heat in 10.6 seconds, equalling the Olympic record. This was excellent news. He had outperformed all his American rivals on time and could go into the semi-final with confidence. For the first time, Harold began to believe that he could win the gold medal.

The Semi-Final and Final were scheduled for the following day and the atmosphere was building nicely. The local newspapers generally favoured Jackson Scholz to take Gold. But Harold had rested well and was ready for a big contest. He had worked extremely hard to get this far and was in great shape. He was going to mount a supreme effort to win this race.

The Semi-Final was set for 4 pm. Harold was up against the American Charlie Paddock, the Canadian Cayofee and the Australian Edwin "Slip" Carr. Having prepared their starting positions, the athletes settled to their marks and then moved to the "set" position. Just as the gun was about to go, Edwin Carr took off to a flying start and was followed instantly by the other athletes – all, that is, apart from Harold himself who was left momentarily on the starting line. Harold reacted quickly but was immediately two yards down on the entire field. With huge focus and determination Harold focussed on staying controlled and relaxed so as not to tighten and thereby lose speed and rhythm. Relentlessly chasing the field down, by halfway he was just one yard off the pace. Bit by bit, he clawed his way to the front until, with just yards to go, he made his trademark dip for the line. As he crossed the finishing line, he was sure he could feel the string at the finishing line against his torso. Had he qualified for the final? Had he perhaps even won the race?

There was an agonising wait for the results. After some minutes, the French announcer made clear that Harold had indeed won the race. Not only that, he had equalled the Olympic record for the second time in the competition. Harold could not be happier. If he could win the semi-final from behind when the entire field had effectively false-started, he could surely win the final on even terms. Harold's confidence climbed. He was ready.

CHAPTER 7

The 100 Metres Final

"Sport at the top is mentally complex. When you need an iron will, when the fires are fiercest, the catalyst can often be your own doubts. However, the best performances in life, whatever you do, can stem from a conflict inside you, from a combination of a sense of imminent failure. And the need to prove, to yourself and other people, that you're not really afraid at all." Lord Coe

HOTEL FRANKLIN

RUE BOUFFAULT

PARIS

JULY 7TH 1924

DEAR MR. ABRAHAMS,

YOU MUST PLEASE PARDON MY NOT COMING TO SEE YOU, MUCH AS I WOULD LIKE TO DO SO.

HOWEVER – I BELIEVE AND HOPE YOU WILL WIN THE 100 METRES. GO OUT DETERMINED TO DO YOUR BEST AND DON'T FORGET TO GO DOWN AT THE FIRST STRIDE.

A SPONGE AND SOME COLD OR PREFERABLY ICED WATER USED AROUND THE NAPE OF THE NECK, UNDER THE EARS AND AT THE WRISTS AND ELBOWS WILL BRACE YOU UP.

GET NICELY WARMED UP AND THEN REACT TO THE GUN.

I SHOULD USE THE SPRINGY OLD 6-SPIKED SHOES.

ALL THE BEST OF LUCK FROM

YOURS TRULY

S.A. MUSSABINI

P.S. PLEASE WISH FRED GABY GOOD LUCK FROM ME.

The men's 100 metres final was scheduled for 7:05 PM and this was Harold's appointment with destiny. If he won, he could draw on this supreme achievement for the rest of his life. But if he lost, he would forever live in the shadow of defeat. It might be just another race to some. But to Harold, it was a defining moment in his life. It meant everything to him. He had poured years of training and resolve into this one moment and now the brutal reality was clear: in just 10 seconds, the outcome would be known and Harold's Olympic destiny would be sealed.

But the semi-final had only just concluded and Harold had another battle to win first. That was the battle with his mind over the next three hours in the build-up to the final. On several previous occasions, Harold had found the nervous tension so great that it had either hindered his performances or he had had to seek reassurance from others to get his confidence back. If that could happen at a domestic competition such as the Oxford versus Cambridge Varsity Match, how could Harold possibly control his nerves in the cauldron of an Olympic final?

Harold had one thing in his favour: he did not consider himself the favourite for the race. The local newspapers agreed with this assessment, with most commentators of the view that the title would go to one of the four Americans – Charley Paddock, Jackson Scholz, Chester Bowman or Loren Murchison. It was clear from the early rounds that Harold would give them a run for their money. But few felt that Harold could actually defeat them. Harold's underdog status suited him. Whereas Harold's position as the leading British sprinter made him feel great pressure to win, this pressure was absent now that the stakes had risen.

Harold had one other trick up his sleeve. He had pre-arranged to spend time with Sam Mussabini in this crucial interim period before the final. Sam's status as a professional coach meant that he could not be present at the Colombes stadium itself.

But Harold had taken the liberty of renting a small hut close to the stadium. Harold had to do this very much on the quiet: Sam's presence would not play well with the British Olympic authorities were it to become known. But for Harold, it was a crucial part of the jigsaw puzzle if he was to stand a chance of winning. And Harold now knew that he had every chance.

Just after the semi-final results were announced, Harold put his plan into play. He also invited the New Zealand sprinter Arthur Porritt to join him – somehow, Harold felt it would help to share the time ahead with one of the other finalists. They made their way over to the hut where Sam was waiting. Away from the excitement of the stadium, it was easier to relax and they could both listen to Sam's calming words of authority. Sam knew exactly how to put Harold into the right frame of mind and instil in him the self-confidence which is so essential to elite performance. By the time the two sprinters left the hut, they were both in the best possible state of mind for the race ahead. They were nervous, but not overly so, and had just that amount of adrenalin necessary for pulling out a top performance.

Back in the stadium, the atmosphere was beginning to build. The Prince of Wales, who would later become King Edward VIII, paid a visit to Harold and Arthur Porritt in a holding room at the stadium. The two sprinters felt much the better for it. Meanwhile, the four American sprinters were having some discussion about a deliberate plan to unsettle Harold. If they each deliberately false started, then by the time the race actually got under way, then maybe – just maybe – Harold's nerves would be sufficiently frayed to undermine his race. Would the Americans really countenance such a ploy? Time would soon tell.

At around 7pm, the Colombes stadium slowly began to fall silent and a heady mixture of excitement and nervousness filled the air. Charley Paddock occupied lane one on the inside of the track. Jackson Scholz occupied lane 2 and Loren Murchison was in lane three. Harold took lane four, a lucky number for him. Chester Bowman was in five and finally, nearest the crowd, Arthur Porritt took lane six. Each sprinter carefully dug out their starting holes in the cinder track. Harold had spent considerable time perfecting this aspect of his race preparation. With exactly the right depth into the ground and positioning away from the start line, these starting holes would give Harold the ability to drive fast and hard when the gun went. It was one element of the crucial first phase of the race.

Perhaps strangely, given his previous form on big occasions, Harold's nerves were not getting to him. This was despite vociferous support from the American section of the crowd. The Americans were noticeably aggressive and keen to show the world that, as in previous Olympics, they had the best sprinters. But somehow, this did not bother Harold: on the contrary, it brought out the warrior instinct in him.

As the sprinters settled down into they starting holes, the crowd hushed completely. The starter, Dr Moir from England, settled them efficiently and they were ready to race. "Pret" came the retort from the starter, signalling the ready position. The sprinters assumed the crouch position from which they would launch their bids for Olympic glory.

The gun went and all sprinters got cleanly away. There had been no false start from the Americans and this would be a fair race. For the first 25 metres, nothing separated the field at all: they ran almost in line. Porritt then began to fall back a little but at the halfway point, there was still nothing to separate Harold and the Americans. Then, magically, Harold began to put some daylight between himself and the rest. For the British supporters and journalists in the crowd, it could not have been more exciting: could Great Britain really have, for the first ever time, a 100 metres Olympic champion? As Harold closed on the line, another piece of drama unfolded as Porritt suddenly started to close on everyone. With thirty metres to go, Harold's arms were pumping for all they were worth and his legs were following. He held his form beautifully and lunged for the line. With a roar from the crowd, Harold crossed the line in clear gold medal position. Scholz took second and Porritt had managed to get himself up into third position.

Harold had, in the process, equalled the Olympic record again by running 10.6 seconds. In fact, one of the timers showed he had run 10.52 seconds but the prevailing rules required that time to be rounded up to 10.6 seconds. But however you looked at it, it was a fast time coming as it did so quickly after the semi-final. All the work with Sam and those long hours of training paid off in those few seconds. Harold had his prize. It was not the Olympic record, which would be beaten in due course anyway. It was the gold medal for that one Olympic race. Nothing could ever take that away.

It had been a remarkable journey for Harold because, in progressing successfully through the various rounds of competition, he had managed to tap untold reserves of mental strength. He later reflected that:

"It wasn't until the semi-final when I was left one and a half yards down that I knew, absolutely knew, I could win. When I won my semi-final in 10 3/5 seconds and Scholz won the other semi-final in 10 4/5 seconds, I knew that I would certainly win the final. I knew at that moment I would win the Olympic final, and four hours later I was lucky enough to do so. I got much more satisfaction in retrospect from my running in the semi-final than I ever did in the final."

Much of the crowd was pleased to see a non-American win. It was refreshing to have another nation take the crown. Harold himself, whilst obviously pleased, had a slightly subdued look. Perhaps he could not quite absorb the moment of his big victory – it was, after all, life-changing for him. Eric had quite some act to follow.

CHAPTER 8

The Second Encounter

In his moment of glory, Harold was generous in his praise of Sam Mussabini. Given Sam's status as a professional coach, there was considerable risk in being quite as outspoken as Harold was when telling reporters:

"Please make it clear that the credit of my win is due to the coaching and genius of Mr Mussabini, the greatest trainer of sprinters in England. Without our combined effort, the result accomplished would never have been achieved. He has encouraged me very much during the last six months and made me stick to it when I sometimes felt inclined to neglect serious efforts."

The various reporters were, for their part, mixed in their assessment of Harold. Several commentators reflected on his lurching style and were also critical of his drop finish. Eric Liddell himself, comparing Harold's style with that of Scholz and Paddock, noted that:

"If you watch the trio in action you will probably think that Abrahams is the more laboured of the three; he seems to expend more energy to get the desired result, yet this fact serves only to confirm his real greatness.....Scholz may have been a sweeter mover, with more rhythm and balance, and Paddock may have been more machine-like in his stride but, when it came to a fight, Abrahams was supreme."

It was perhaps the case that Harold won despite his style but it was no less an achievement for that. The British Olympic Association held a celebration dinner in Paris with the Prince of Wales as the guest of honour. General Charles Sherrill, the US representative on the International Olympic Committee, was invited and spoke generously of Harold's victory. Amongst the British athletes, the praise was somewhat muted. Harold remained a relatively unpopular member of the team, having been so openly critical in the press of them just weeks before the Olympics. He had, in any event, not been popular among his fellow Cambridge University athletes and there were several on the Olympic team.

Harold himself had no time to celebrate his victory in any serious way for he had more work to do: the opening rounds of the 200 metres followed immediately the next day. Harold started convincingly, beating the American Charley Paddock in the first round in 22.2 seconds. He followed this up with another victory in the second round, this time beating the American Bayes Norton in 22.0 seconds exactly. It was in the semi-final that the magnitude of Harold's task became clearer, for Harold was beaten into third place by Jackson Scholz and George Hill of the USA. Was the sheer volume and intensity of Harold's race schedule beginning to take its toll? Or could Harold muster one last individual effort to claim double Olympic victory?

Eric also progressed through the early rounds comfortably enough. He won his first around heat in 22.2 seconds and finished second to the Australian Slip Carr in the next round. In the semi-final Eric finished second again. And so, for the second time in their careers, Harold and Eric were to face off to each other. And there could be no more enthralling occasion than the Olympic 200 metres final.

As the runners settled into their starting positions, hopes remained high that Harold could once again defeat the much fancied Americans. But as the runners set off, it was the American Charley Paddock who set off at a blistering pace. After 100 metres, Paddock was still ahead but was being pursued determinedly by a chasing group which included Eric. Harold himself was a further yard or so off the pace. As they neared the finish, Paddock made the mistake of looking back. It is a tactic which never reaps reward. In the final yards of the race, despite Paddock's lunge for the tape, Scholz sped past and took victory in 21.7 seconds. Paddock took second and Eric took a deserved third in 21.9 seconds. Harold, meanwhile, trailed in last in 6th place. It had been one race too many for Harold – and one race where the tactics he had agreed with Sam had simply failed. Sam had suggested that, in the semi-final, Harold had set off too quickly. Sam therefore suggested that Harold start conservatively in the final itself, conserving his energy for the latter stages of the race. The plan backfired – Harold effectively lost the race in the first fifty metres when Paddock started at a pace which left Harold with too much ground to recover in the latter stages. Harold reflected ruefully after the event:

"When we entered the straight, I was well down and I finished a very bad sixth. I have always regretted that I did not run better in that 200 metres. Naturally the reaction after the 100 metres was to be expected. I still believe that I was better over 200 than 100. If only I could run that 200 metres again!"

Eric himself had pronounced views on Harold's performance and his merits as a runner compared to Scholz. He did not share Harold's views about his relative superiority over the longer distance:

"He finished last, quite run out, and his defeat rather confirms my suspicion that his style takes a heavy toll on his physical attributes, especially over a distance greater than 100 yards. Scholz, on the other hand, seems to take less out of himself and keeps his balance better. This was not enough when he just went under to Abrahams in the "hundred" because Abrahams had the will to win and was able to maintain it until the finish; over the longer distance, however, the stylist prevailed."

Some years later, Harold reflected on his rivalry with Eric:

"I never ran against him in a 100. I ran against him in a 200 and he beat me. He beat me but I think I was a better sprinter than him, actually. At this long distance from the actual event I can perhaps say, without seeming self-centred, that I believe I was, in fact, better than Eric over 100 metres – though it is equally fair to say that, in the only two occasions that I ran against him (over 220 yards and 200 metres), he defeated me. In the final, he finished third behind Scholz and Paddock, beating two other Americans G.L. Hill and B.M. Norton in the process. Liddell was a pretty fair way ahead of me. I was last."

Was it really true to say that Harold was the better sprinter? Harold asserted his superiority but, many years after he made the above comments, he did not seem quite so certain:

"I have often wondered whether I owe my Olympic success, at least in part, to Eric's religious beliefs. Had he run in that event, would he have defeated me and won that Olympic title?"

Others held Harold in higher regard than he apparently held himself. For example, Philip Noel-Baker, Britain's 1920 and 1924 Olympic captain, said:

"I have always believed that Harold Abrahams was the only European sprinter who could have run with Jesse Owens, Ralph Metcalfe, and the other great sprinters from the US. He was in their class, not only because of natural gifts – his magnificent physique, his splendid racing temperament, his flair for the big occasion; but because he understood athletics and had given more brainpower and more will power to the subject than any other runner of his day."

But the fair answer is that we shall never know who would have been the better sprinter in the 1924 Olympic 100 metres final. And the 200 metres Olympic final was to be the last time Harold and Eric would ever race each other. It was now time for Eric to take centre stage in an event which, a year earlier, he barely had any pedigree. What could he make of it in the fierce heat of Olympic competition?

CHAPTER 9

The 400 Metres Final

"I run the first 200 metres as hard as I can. Then, for the second 200 metres, with God's help, I run harder."

The preliminary rounds of the 400 metres took place on Thursday 10 July. Eric won his first round heat comfortably in 50.2 seconds. He also progressed easily into the semi-final when he finished second to the Dutch athlete Paulen in the second round. These were comfortable and convincing runs. But it was very difficult to know how Eric would fare against the best in the world. The Swiss runner Imbach had run 48 seconds to establish a new World and Olympic record. How could Eric contain that kind of speed? It seemed to be in a different class. Furthermore, some felt that his ungainly style might not stand up to multiple rounds of competition at this level. Harold observed that:

"Liddell's style was quite the most unorthodox ever, with arms revolving like the sails of a windmill, head thrust back and an exaggerated knee lift. People are apt to ask whether he would not have been an even greater runner if he had possessed a more polished style. In theory the answer is 'yes' but often in trying to impose a style on a runner you ruin his individuality and spoil his performance."

But the key to understanding Eric's greatness as an athlete lies not in matters of running style. It was his closeness to God which defined him. Eric ran not for individual glory or even for the glory of his country. He ran as an expression of his love of and belief in God. And in so doing, he naturally acquired the mind-set of a champion. For in each race he would run with God's will and with the all-consuming belief that he would deliver his very best performance, whatever that might be on the day. Not for Eric the personal anxieties which attended Harold. Rather, each race was a manifestation of his relationship with God.

Having had two encouraging runs in the opening rounds, the British camp began to entertain the possibility of success for Eric.

Harold was, like many others, caught up in the excitement of the occasion:

"When we went back to the hotel on the Thursday evening of July 10, 1924, we had hopes that Liddell might win the 400 metres final on the morrow. But we had to confess that he had not to date done anything like 48.0 seconds for the distance. Indeed, his best was almost a second slower."

When Eric left the team hotel, the Hotel Moderne, on the day of the final rounds, one of the British support team handed him a note. Eric read the note when he got to the Colombes Stadium. It read as follows:

"It says in the Old Book, 'Him that honours me, I will honour.' Wishing you the best of success always."

Eric had total conviction that he had been right to avoid competing in the 100 m on Sunday. However, as a result, he had received much criticism from many quarters. This note, however, encouraged him and reinforced his belief that he was doing the right thing.

The semi-finals took place at 3pm on Friday July 11. The first semi-final was won by the American Fitch, who further improved the World and Olympic record to 47.8 seconds. Butler of Great Britain took second and the Canadian Johnson was third. Eric won the second semi-final comfortably, beating the Swiss runner Imbach into second, with the American Taylor third. Eric recorded a time of 48.2 seconds in that race, a time which put him within easy reach of the fastest at the Games. For the first time, British supporters could believe that Eric might be very competitive in the final.

The final was run at 6pm, exactly three hours after the semi-final. As a competitor, Harold was entitled to a seat in the stadium. But the allocated seat did not afford a particularly good view of the finish, so Harold paid ten shillings to get a better view.

Eric was drawn in the outside lane. This is generally considered to be the worst possible lane in the 400 metres, because it means you are unable to chart the progress of the other runners in the race and gauge your own effort accordingly. Johnson of Canada was drawn on the inside lane, with Guy Butler from Great Britain in lane two. Imbach, the Swiss athlete, was in lane three and the American, Coard Taylor, was running in line four. Horatio Fitch was in lane five, right next to Eric.

As the gun went and the crowd roared, Eric immediately set off at a frighteningly fast pace. Harold recalled that:

"From the crack of the pistol Liddell ran like a man inspired. He dashed off with all the frenzy of a sprinter."

Most onlookers felt that Liddell would "blow up", having failed to judge his pace appropriately. By the halfway point, Eric led by 3 metres and seemed to be running at full speed. In fact, Eric had gone through 200 metres in 22.2 seconds: this was significantly faster than world record pace and it was clear that he could not continue at such a pace for the entire race. But then neither could anyone else. After a further 100 metres, Eric was still in the lead when Imbach stumbled and fell to the track, unable to continue. Eric sped on, unaware that this had happened.

As the runners came down the home straight, Fitch tried to narrow the gap on Eric, thinking that Eric would necessarily slow down as the finishing line approached. But Eric threw his head back in one final burst of determination and burst through the finishing line to take a glorious victory by a clear 5 metres. Eric had completed the distance in 47.2 seconds, a new world record.

Eric's achievement was nothing short of astonishing. The year before, Eric had been a 100 metres and 200 metres specialist. It was only relatively recently, in Olympic year itself, that he had picked up the 400 metres at all. And going into the Olympics, Eric clearly did not have world-class pedigree in the event. But now, on Friday, July 11, 1924, Eric was Olympic champion and world record holder. It was a record that was to stand for some years.

Horatio Fitch later wrote a charming tribute to Eric:

"Tho a sprinter by practice, he ran the pick of the world's quarter milers off their feet. Tho a small man, he makes his legs move fast enuf to beat his rangy competitors. His form is all wrong by our standards, for he runs almost leaning back, and his chin is almost pointing to heaven, yet he won his race on pluck and stamina. And most difficult of all, he had to set his own pace all the way, where one instant's faltering judgement would have meant defeat."

Meanwhile, Harold himself was full of praise and admiration for Eric's finest achievement, choosing these simple words:

"Eric's brilliant victory at the Paris Olympiad will always remain an epic."

Beyond The Olympics

CHAPTER 10

Homecoming: Harold

"I cannot speak with experience of any section of the Games but the purely athletic one, and here a whole week's programme was carried out with hardly a single minute of unpleasantness…..the spirit of true sportsmanship was wonderful." Harold Abrahams defending the Olympic movement.

Harold and Eric were the heroes of the hour but when the crowds met the British team train at London's Victoria station, Harold was nowhere to be seen. Eric was carried shoulder high to a nearby taxi but Harold was not there to enjoy a similar gesture. Arthur Porritt, Harold's new friend and a Rhodes scholar who was travelling with the British team, recalled:

"He didn't come home with us. I think he was just terribly emotional. He was just overcome by having achieved his objective and also he was completely deflated mentally, worn out."

Harold had decided to take a few days' holiday in Paris. He had no particular need to rush home and the prospect of a few days' holiday seemed rather appealing by contrast. In any event, when he did get back to London, Harold was still very much the man of the moment. For example, he and Eric were both guests at a dinner in the House of Commons at the end of July.

The British public was keen to see its Olympic heroes in action and a match had been organised between the British Empire and the Americans at Stamford Bridge. Harold did not run well, however, and it seems likely that Arthur Porritt's analysis – Harold's emotional exhaustion – was the reason. It is not uncommon for newly-crowned Olympic champions to experience such feelings: at once, the major driving force of the athlete's existence is removed and a sense of empty desolation can descend instead. In any event, the crowd of between 30,000 and 40,000 left rather disappointed at Harold's performance. Harold subsequently wrote about it:

"There have been many different descriptions about the 400 [4 x 100] yards relay which the Americans won in the world record time of 37 4/5 seconds. The true facts are these: I ran the last stage and owing to a big error on my part, did not start to run at the proper time, so that W. P. Nichol, who was handing over to me, had to slow down for fear of passing lane. As he did not seem to be catching me I hesitated, and a man in two minds in a race of less than 100 yards is no good to anyone. When I did get the baton I was well behind Leconey. The error of judgement was due to lack of practice. The British Empire team had never once been together before. In a short relay like 4 x 100 yards the changeover is everything. And it takes a good deal of hard work to perfect this branch of athletics."

Later that summer there was a further opportunity for Harold to test himself. The Achilles club were to take on the British Dominions at the Queen's Club. Eric would not compete because he had no affiliation to either of these teams. But on this occasion Harold was beaten in the 100 yards by Arthur Porritt, who later said:

"I beat him on that occasion, within a fortnight of him getting a gold medal at the Olympics. It shows that he was tired out. I was on top of the world achieving what I did."

As a consequence, his brother Adolphe, the doctor, advised him not to run for a year. There were rumours at the time that Harold had suffered some kind of breakdown but such rumours were denied.

Nonetheless, Harold kept himself very busy in that summer of 1924. For one thing, he set himself the task of defending the Olympic movement itself. The 1924 Olympic Games had finished in an unsatisfactory manner. In the rugby final, when the USA defeated France, a riot had ensued and American players and fans had been attacked. Furthermore, there had been incidents of foul play in fencing and boxing. With all of this as background, Harold took to the pages of the Sunday Express on August 3, 1924:

"A great deal has been written in the past few days on "whether the Olympic Games are a good or bad thing". Certainly no good can come of whitewashing the unpleasant incidents which undoubtedly did take place, but only harm can result from the attempt which has been made to suggest that these incidents are typical of the animosity which permeates the whole games.

Now, because "unpleasant incidents" have occurred in three of the eighteen Olympic sports, it is suggested: "The events have shown the world is not right for such a brotherhood" as Baron Pierre de Coubertin, who was responsible for the revival of the Olympic Games, anticipated.

Because the French nation, or a section of it, forgot themselves at a Rugby football match, because one or two fencers displayed a lack of character and indulged in petulant and childish outbursts of anger, because a Frenchman confused boxing with biting, we are asked to endorse the suggestion that the Olympic Games are a bad thing, and that we should cease to take part in them.

I cannot speak with experience of any section of the Games but the purely athletic one, and here a whole week's programme was carried out with hardly a single minute of unpleasantness. There was stupidity over a walking race, but otherwise the spirit of true sportsmanship was wonderful. It would be a calamity if the athletic section of the Games – the pure Olympic Games – did not take place."

Some had questioned whether the Olympics should ever take place again. Harold's influential intervention did much to ensure that they did.

CHAPTER 11

Homecoming: Eric

"In the dust of defeat as well as in the laurels of victory there is a glory to be found if one has done his best." Eric Liddell

While he was preparing for the Olympics, Eric had got used to the idea of being a public figure and a well-known Scottish athlete. However, the reception that greeted him on his return from the Olympics took him greatly by surprise.

D.P. Thompson was absolutely thrilled with Eric's Olympic victory. He could immediately see that Eric's Olympic success would be a great attraction for young people who had little interest in Christianity but who would nonetheless be willing to listen to Eric speaking. Thompson was not going to miss out on this opportunity to market Eric's success. On Monday July 14, as the Great Britain team returned by ferry across the English Channel, an article appeared in the Glasgow Herald by D.P. Thompson with the headline "E. H. Liddell: Scotland's Olympic hero." The article concluded as follows:

"The announcement that Liddell is to preach in the Scottish Kirk at Paris (that event took place yesterday) serves as a reminder that our champion's main interest does not lie on the athletic field. To multitudes who know little of football or running, the name of E.H. Liddell is fast becoming known as a speaker to young men, whose presence in the pulpit or on the platform serves as a reminder that the finest athletic prowess often goes hand in hand with enthusiastic and effective spiritual work. Liddell's career on the running track may be drawing to a close, but his great work among young people in the interest of a vital and wholehearted Christian discipleship is only just beginning, and the effects of that work are likely to be as far-reaching as the fruits are great. China is the goal Liddell has in front of him and having completed his science course at Edinburgh University, he looks forward to a period of combined theological training and evangelistic campaigning before following his brother out to the mission field. "

Just days after Eric arrived back in Edinburgh, his graduation ceremony from Edinburgh University took place. Along with hundreds of other students, Eric took his place in McEwan Hall for the University's graduation ceremony. When Eric stood to receive his Bachelor's degree, applause spontaneously broke out among students and fellows alike. By the time he climbed onto the platform to receive his degree, everyone had got up to give Eric a standing ovation. The ovation continued until Sir Alfred Ewing called for quiet.

Sir Alfred spoke directly to Eric: "Mr Liddell, you have shown that none can pass you except the examiners. In the ancient Olympic contests the victor was crowned with wild olive by the High Priest of Zeus and a poem composed in his honour was presented to him. The Vice Chancellor is no High Priest, but he speaks and acts for the University; and in the name of the University which is proud of you, and to which you have brought fresh honour, I present you with this epigram in Greek, composed by Professor Mair and I also place upon your brow this chaplet of wild olive."

After the graduation ceremony, Eric was carried shoulder high by fellow students to Saint Giles Cathedral on the Royal Mile for a special post-graduation service. Eric was asked to give a speech and he chose typically modest words:

"When I was in America earlier this year I saw written over the entrance of the University of Pennsylvania: "In the dust of defeat as well as in the laurels of victory there is a glory to be found if one has done his best." There are many here who have done their best, though they haven't succeeded in gaining the laurels of victory. To all such, there is as much honour due as to those who have received the laurels of victory."

Eric was, without doubt, universally popular among the students. To give some idea of just how popular, here is what an article in the Edinburgh University paper, The Student, said about him:

"Success in athletics sufficient to turn the head of an ordinary man has left Liddell absolutely unspoilt, and his modesty is entirely genuine and unaffected. He has taken his triumph in his stride, as it were, and never made any sort of fuss. What he has thought it right to do, that he has done, looking neither to the left nor to the right, and yielding not one jot or tittle of principle either to court applause or to placate criticism. Courteous and affable, he is utterly free from gush. Devoted to his principles, he is without a touch of Pharisaism. The best that can be said of any student is that he has left the fame of his university fairer than he found it, and his grateful alma mater is proud to recognise that to no man does that praise more certainly belong than to Eric Henry Liddell."

The celebrations continued the following day at a "complimentary dinner" held in Mackie's Dining Saloon on Princes Street, the main street in Edinburgh's so-called new town. Most of Edinburgh society attended. The dinner was chaired by Lord Sands and other attendees included the Lord Provost, Sir William Sleigh, the Principal of the University, Sir Alfred Ewing, and numerous other dignitaries and clergymen. The menu card stated simply:

"In admiration of his remarkable athletic achievements, and to his devotion to principle in that connection as a reverent upholder of the Christian Sabbath."

Lord Sands greatly admired Eric and the stand he had taken in refusing to run the 100 metres at the Olympics. In his opening remarks, Lord Sands made clear what he thought:

"In these days of moral flabbiness, it is something to find a man who is not content to shield himself behind such easy phrases as, "It is only once in the way" or, "When you go to Rome, you must do as they do in Rome.""

When it was Eric's turn to speak, he referred to the note that the team physio had given him on the day of the 400 metres finals: "It says in the Old Book, 'Him that honours me, I will honour.' Wishing you the best of success always." For Eric, this moment was a highlight of the Games.

At the end of the meeting, it was decided to send a cable to Eric's parents in China and it read as follows:

"Large gathering, Edinburgh, chairman Lord Sands cordially congratulates father and mother on Eric's wonderful feat and still more on his noble witness for Christian principles."

As soon as the dinner was over, Eric headed to Waverley station in the centre of Edinburgh to take the train down to London for, on the following day, there was a relay match between the British Empire and the USA. The meeting took place at Stamford Bridge and was very much dominated by the American athletes.

However, the 4 x 440 yards relay included a strong team from the British Empire and was much anticipated by the crowd. The British Empire team comprised Edward Toms on the first leg, Richard Ripley on the second leg, Guy Butler on the third leg and Eric on the anchor leg. The Americans also had a strong team: there were three individuals who had competed in the 400 metres at the Olympics – Eric Wilson, Ray Robinson and Horatio Fitch – along with Bill Stevenson, the Rhodes scholar from Oxford.

The race was evenly contested but, coming into the final lap, Fitch had a comfortable lead of some six yards. This was a significant gap for Eric to close down: Fitch was the man who had taken the silver medal in Paris. Eric set off in determined pursuit and, by the time he had got to the end of the back straight, he had caught up most of the ground. Fitch maintained his lead going into the home straight but could not hold off Eric who stormed past to take victory by some three yards. The 400 metres relay was one of only two victories out of eight races that afternoon and was just 1/5 of a second outside the world record at that time. It established Eric as the clear world leader at the event. Harold later recalled the achievement with great generosity:

"10 days later, before a record crowd at Stamford Bridge, he again showed an astonishing resolution when, as anchor man and against Fitch, one of America's finest quarter-milers, he turned an appreciable deficiency into a three yard victory. There is no man in the world other than Liddell who could give six yards to a crack American quarter-miler who has recorded 48 1/10, and beat him. The thunderous applause from the crowd of over 30,000 at Stamford Bridge as Liddell, his arms and legs working like some great helicopter, caught his man, still sound in my ears whenever I hear the race. The excitement of the crowd as Liddell, with his arms radiating like an animated windmill and his head thrust right back, overhauled his American opponent at the last bend to win was tremendous. The applause they gave him was a combined acknowledgement of his magnificent win for Britain in Paris, his phenomenal victory that afternoon, and his popularity as a great sportsman. The relay meeting showed the British public first, how exciting relay racing can be, and second, how real is the friendship between the athletes of the British Empire and the United States. Liddell's quarter must have been something in the region of 48 seconds. It was his last race in England (though he did win three Scottish titles in 1925). It was the last time I ever saw him run. The following year, he left for China to carry out his life work as a missionary. No words can describe Liddell's running and the passing years did not dim the picture of that indomitable courage."

CHAPTER 12

The Elder Statesman of UK Athletics

"The whole of his subsequent life depended on the fact that he'd won the Olympic 100 metres." Sir Arthur Porritt.

With his Olympic 100 metres victory behind him, doors opened in Harold's life for ever more. Harold himself said:

"I think my own good luck in winning has made a tremendous difference to my whole life. I like to feel that if I had been second by 6 inches I would still have managed to achieve a number of things I've been happy to achieve, but they don't say how much you're second by… The winner is outstanding in people's minds; far more importance is attached to winning than I believe ought to be attached, but that's human nature."

Harold's competitive career ended rather abruptly in May 1925. The occasion was a match between Bedford County and the London Athletic Club at Stamford Bridge in London. Harold had already finished second in the long jump but had chosen to do another jump in front of a group of photographers. Harold recalled the occasion vividly:

"The long jump and run-up at Stamford Bridge had been used a great deal of the day before by a lot of schoolboys and the take-off was very badly worn. I ran up to the take-off board, I took off and my take-off leg trailed instead of coming up to meet the other one. I think I must have twisted it. Anyway I went straight into the ground at about 15, 16 or 17 miles per hour with a straight leg. I heard a noise, rather like Smee tearing up a bit of sailcloth in Peter Pan. I heard this, didn't realise that it belonged to me, and I passed out. The pain was so acute that I just passed out. I broke my leg, tore badly through a lot of muscles. My leg was nearly doubled up. When I got up my leg was all bent and I had to be carried. I think I was actually carried off the track to the dressing room on a hurdle."

It was not until the following day that a leading London surgeon advised Harold: "I can operate. But if I do there is a risk that you'll lose your leg."

Harold's reaction, perhaps surprisingly, was one of relief:

"That was the end, so far as athletics was concerned. I'll be absolutely truthful, I laid back there and I said, "This is marvellous." I was very uncertain about what to do in athletics, and here I had no option, my mind had been made up for me. What did I think of it? Strangely, my first reaction was of relief, outweighing any disappointment. I was faced no more with any problem of when to retire."

For others there was disappointment. Evelyn Montague, for one, believed that Harold would have gone on to achieve still greater things:

"In actual fact, he had only begun to realise his full capabilities. I firmly believe that, if he had not broken down, he would have won both the 100 and 200 metres at the 1928 Olympic Games, and would have proved himself one of the three or four greatest sprinters of all time."

But Harold seemed to put his enforced retirement behind him very quickly and set about his new life with all the energy and ambition that had marked him out as an athlete. Norris McWhirter, one of the original co-writers of the Guinness Book of Records, commented that "Harold Abrahams raised athletics from a minor to a major national sport." He also made a significant contribution as a public servant for the National Parks Commission. So there is no question that Harold left a considerable legacy. And he was also a man for whom, despite his numerous work commitments, the family unit was to be cherished.

Harold as Sports Commentator

One of Harold's first pursuits was sports commentary work and he was one of the very first to commentate on live radio. He did his first radio commentary in 1926 and in March 1927, he broadcast live on the Varsity athletics match between Oxford and Cambridge at the Queen's Club. This was the first ever outside broadcast of a sporting event. Harold was well cut out for the role since he had, as Norris McWhirter[3] noted, a fine speaking voice and exemplary preparation:

"Harold possessed one of the finest speaking voices in the country. Those wonderful articulated and modulated words of his and his meticulous statistical preparation set a standard and comprised a whole technique of live commentary and summary on which the BBC's reputation as the world's premier sports service can justly be said to have been founded."

In 1936, Harold commentated for the BBC on the Berlin Olympics which were famously presided over by Adolf Hitler. This cemented his reputation as a skilled and erudite commentator. It was ironic, therefore, that there had been much internal wrangling at the BBC, who had put pressure on Harold not to go. There was concern over the fact that he was a Jew by origin and that, by sending him, controversy might ensue.

---

[3] Norris McWhirter was one of the co-writers of The Guinness Book of Records.

On December 5, 1935, one of the BBC Managers, Lotbiniere, wrote to his bosses and tried to be supportive of Harold:

"You will remember that at the Programme Board meeting in the late autumn we discussed the advisability of using Mr Abrahams as our commentator at the Olympic Games. It was then found that, while we were not prejudiced against him for racial reasons, it might be advisable to postpone the final decision as to his appointment by us until nearer the time, when we should be able to see the state of feeling in Germany, and the consequent probability of their differentiating against him in the matter of facilities.

Mr Abrahams came to see me a few days ago, and while he had no wish to force us into a decision that we did not wish to make, he said that it would be a great help to him to know whether he was likely to be our official commentator....

In these circumstances, and recollecting the Foreign Director's expressed conviction that they would never dare to interfere in any way with our commentator, I should now like to know if we could give him the use of our name.

S. J. de Lotbiniere."

On December 6, 1935, Cecil Graves, the BBC Programme Controller wrote very directly as follows:

"The point about this is, of course, that Abrahams is a Jew. He is our best commentator on athletics. Apparently if we are prepared to come out into the open and label him the BBC commentator for the Olympic Games, he's quite ready to go to Germany.

The question arises as to whether we should do this. We all regard the German action against the Jews as quite irrational and intolerable and on that score we ought not to hesitate, but should we, as between one broadcaster and another, put aside all views of this kind and take the line that however irrational we regard another country's attitude to be, it would be discourteous to send a Jewish commentator to a country where Jews are taboo?

My own reaction is that we should write to the German broadcasting people and tell them that our own expert man, whom we are proposing to send to the Olympic Games, is Mr Abrahams and leave them to raise any objection if they want to. I made some enquiries about the reception accorded to a member of a recent delegation to Germany who was a Jew and I was told that he was very well received and the was no question of any discourtesy or unpleasantness.

C. G. Graves, December 6, 1935"

Harold himself was extremely keen to make the trip and took steps proactively to manage towards this outcome. In particular, Harold had boldly sought and secured a meeting with Hans von Tschammer und Osten, who was Hitler's Sports Fuhrer, and whose displays at Nazi rallies shamelessly promoted the superiority of the " race. Harold wrote to Lotbiniere on the matter:

"My dear de Lotbiniere,
It will interest you to know that last week I had an interview of nearly half an hour with Herr von Tschammer und Osten, and among other things he gave me his personal assurance that I would be *welcome* in Berlin next year at the Olympic Games.

I gave him my personal undertaking that I would not disclose to the Press the fact of our interview, so that you will appreciate that the information given to you is confidential!!!!!!

Yours ever,

Harold M. Abrahams."

Ultimately, in July 1936, the BBC informed the German authorities that the two men selected for staff duty in Berlin would be Mr Alan Wells, a member of the news department, and Tommy Woodruffe of Outside Broadcasts. This followed advice from the German Embassy that it would be "impolitic" to send Harold as the BBC's special commentator. The German Embassy had, however, indicated that Harold could travel to Berlin in some other capacity. It was therefore determined that Harold would travel to Berlin as Assistant Manager to the team.

The challenges that had faced Harold at an individual level were to a large extent mirrored at a national level: there were some who thought it inappropriate for Great Britain to go to the games at all on account of the attitude of the Hitler regime to Jews.

"We must remember that the International Olympic Committee, the body solely responsible for the games, has, rightly or wrongly, decided that it is still the right thing to hold the games in Germany. This body is entrusted with the observance of the Olympic Charter. We must remember that the British Olympic Association, the body responsible for Olympic matters in this country, has decided to support the Games. I have no delusions about the situation in Germany today; and if I had been born in Germany, knowing myself as I do, I doubt if I should be alive today."

Harold went on:

"I still think the right thing is for us to show the German people what Great Britain believes to be real sport. After all, in my opinion, to isolate an individual because his behaviour does not meet with your approval never ultimately achieves anything. Countries are only collections of individuals and to isolate Germany will never achieve what we ultimately want, namely, the furtherance of these ideals in sport – absolute freedom for all to participate – freedom in which we all believe."

And so it was that Harold travelled to Berlin as Assistant Team Manager to the British Olympic Team but nonetheless managed to undertake his much-cherished commentary work. It was the making of his reputation as a commentator.

It was at the Berlin Games that the great black sprinter Jesse Owens sealed his reputation – much to the irritation of Hitler, who preferred to believe in the supremacy of the Aryan race. Harold, though, was quick to recognise the immense talent of Owens and made sure both to meet him and be photographed with him. Harold was in no doubt about the brilliance of Owens:

"I thank my lucky stars this morning, and again this afternoon, that I was not born 12 years later. If I had been I certainly would never have had the proud distinction of winning an Olympic event.

Jesse Owens, the 21-year-old negro from Ohio, is certainly the most beautiful moving human being I have ever seen tearing down a sprint track. But 'tearing' is really the wrong word. He seems to float along in effortless precision, and it is only that he makes his opponents, who themselves are first-class sprinters, look like selling-platers that indicates the glorious speed with which this modest whirlwind traverses the cinder path."

In all, Owens took four gold medals in Berlin – the 100 metres, the 200 metres, the long jump and the 4 x 100 metres. This was exasperating for Hitler but there was nothing he could do about it.

Harold was also much taken with the victory of the New Zealander, Jack Lovelock, in the 1500 metres. Lovelock was a friend of Harold's and, unlike the 100 metres, Harold was given the opportunity to commentate on the race. The drama of the occasion rather got to Harold, with one newspaper commenting:

"For the first three laps he (Abrahams) gave a clear description of the race, but on the fourth lap excitement got the better of him and all he could do was to cheer on Lovelock against his American arrival, Cunningham."

Harold later commented:

"I was so close to Hitler, I could have shot him. I wish I had."

Harold the Family Man

In 1934, Harold met an opera singer called Sybil Evers. She had invited him to her table at Grosvenor House and they immediately struck up a close relationship. It was a whirlwind romance, though at times Sybil made her feelings more clearly known than Harold. In September 1935, Sybil penned the following poem:

I would give you Beauty
Were Beauty mine to give,
And all the happy things of Life
As long as you may live.

The glory of the sunlight,
The laughing summer hours -
The wonder lying 'neath the scent
Of hay, and sun-warmed flowers.

And you should hear the music
Of softly-falling rain,
And watch the ever-changing light
And shadow on the plain.

And I would give you starlight,
With the pale moon above,
And gentle peace, and quietness -
And love.

Harold had some sensitivity to getting married but they eventually did so in a rather rushed ceremony in 1936 after he had found the courage to propose to her.

The Four-minute Mile

Harold first met Roger Bannister on Saturday March 22 1947 at the White City Stadium in London. It was the annual Varsity Match between Oxford and Cambridge Universities. Bannister, representing Oxford, took an easy and surprising victory that day in the mile; it was a race that confirmed in his own mind that he had some talent worth nurturing. For his part, Harold certainly recognised Bannister's physical talent. But he also recognised a highly-strung personality which would need to be both controlled and channelled if Bannister was to achieve the highest performances his talent could deliver. Perhaps Harold even saw a bit of himself in that persona. Banister later wrote in his book " The First Four Minutes " :

"I met (Harold Abrahams) for the first time that evening......(he) has made such a great contribution to the popularity of athletics in this country, both by his writing and broadcasting. On this occasion he noted my promise, and it was the beginning of a close friendship which has continued throughout my athletic career. The advice has been invaluable to me on all occasions when important decisions have had to be made."

After that day in March 1947, Harold took an interest in Bannister's blossoming running career and it was not too long before Harold was making the connection between Bannister and the elusive four-minute mile. After a disappointing experience at the Olympic Games in Helsinki in 1952 – Bannister had finished fourth in the 1,500 metres after unexpectedly having to run an extra qualifying heat – the challenge of breaking the four-minute barrier for the mile became an all-consuming goal for Bannister.

The big day came in Oxford on 6 May 1954 at the Iffley Road track. By this time, as well as having Harold as mentor, Bannister had also enjoyed the benefits of training with Franz Stampfl. Stampfl, an Austrian who had also been coaching Bannister's friends Chris Brasher and Chris Chataway, put them through punishing interval sessions at the Duke of York Barracks in London. The occasion of the attempt was a match between Oxford University and the Amateur Athletic Association, although Bannister and his friends Chataway and Brasher – who were acting as pacemakers – were actually running for the Achilles Club[4]. In the event, the pacing was near perfect and

---

[4] The club was formed in 1920 for past and present members of Cambridge University Athletic Club and Oxford University Athletic Club.

Bannister crossed the line in three minutes 59.4 seconds. Harold was not only present, he subsequently had himself cited as one of the official timekeepers. Given that Harold was not listed in the program as such, it is not clear how Harold was able to do this. Nonetheless, there is absolutely no question that Harold had contributed to Bannister's remarkable feat and, as is clear from the correspondence below, Bannister himself certainly did not question the inclusion of Harold as a timekeeper.

Harold, who was fascinated with timekeeping to the point of obsession, reflected as follows on the four-minute mile:

"I kept on asking myself why. Let's look at the facts, calmly if we can. A runner ran a mile just two seconds faster than anyone else had ever done before. The mile record has been beaten many, many times in the history of sport, but never has a record caused so much excitement. All, really, because that record moved from one side of the whole number four to the other... ... There can be no doubt at all that for all time people will remember that Bannister was the first man to run a four-minute mile."

In recognition of his achievement, Harold gave Roger one of the stopwatches that had been used in the four-minute mile. It was engraved with the words "From Harold Abrahams, timekeeper, presented to Roger Bannister, on the occasion of his four-minute mile."

Roger wrote back to thank Harold for his generous gift:

"My dear Harold,

Your wonderful surprise arrived this morning and I quite literally don't know how to thank you. (I can hear you saying "Don't try!")

You have played such a large part in any success I have achieved – as my guide, philosopher and friend – but it is difficult for me to say enough of what I feel. All I can hope is that we can continue to remain as close when my running days are over!

My father will be using the new watch this afternoon – though at the moment I think he feels it's too precious to touch. I expect I shall see you before you read this but I wanted to write immediately to say how much I was thrilled by your present.

Yours ever,

Roger"

Harold as Public Servant: The National Parks Commission

Somewhat by chance, in 1950, Harold became secretary of a newly-formed body called the National Parks Commission. It was a post he was to hold until 1963. Harold had been working at the Ministry of Town and Country Planning, enjoyed it and was offered a new role to develop the National Parks. It was a job he came to absolutely adore. As his daughter, Sue Pottle, said: "He was absolutely patriotic, all for King and country."

Harold described his task in the following terms:

"The National Parks Commission was set up primarily to designate National Parks. We've got ten of them. Lake District, Peak District, Pembrokeshire Coast, Dartmoor, Exmoor, Northumberland and so on, with the idea that those are areas where the public can enjoy beautiful scenery and get sufficient recreation. It is a frightfully lucky job to have because it brings one into contact with so many people. Local authorities manage the Parks. I go down to Park meetings and help with problems.

You've got a great conflict. You've got a limited amount of land in this country. How is it to be used? Are you to have recreation or are you to have a power station? I am essentially a person who believes that the only way in life is compromise. It doesn't mean giving away on things that really matter. There are precious few things that you can be absolutely certain about. I enjoy enormously trying to bring together two conflicting interests and trying to sort it out… and get those people thoroughly dissatisfied with the result!"

After some ten years in this position, during which his negotiation skills had brought several notable developments in the National Parks, Harold declared:

"I've got a lovely job, one of the nicest jobs I could ever have run into… I've seen more England in the last ten years than I saw in the first fifty."

In 1957, Harold was formally recognised for his work when he was made Commander of the Order of the British Empire. Stanley Matthews, the famous footballer, was among the others to be similarly honoured that year.

Harold as Pioneer and Statesman of UK Athletics

Throughout his life following his retirement from competitive athletics, Harold worked tirelessly – and often on a voluntary basis – for British athletics, serving as administrator, journalist, broadcaster, historian and statistician. It was in these spheres that he made his most obvious mark in addition to his Olympic achievements. He was the athletics correspondent for the Sunday Times from 1925 to 1967 and a founder member of the Association of Track & Field Statisticians. He became a member of the AAA

General Committee in 1926, was appointed Secretary in 1931 and President in 1976. He was also the first Secretary of the International Board, which preceded the British Amateur Athletic Board ('BAAB'), and in 1963 he was appointed Chairman of the BAAB after serving as Treasurer for 21 years.

By the 1950s, he was actively campaigning for women to be included in Olympic fencing from which they were at the time excluded. It is fair to say that he helped to change the face of British athletics in this respect.

Harold was always his own man when it came to opinions about things that really mattered to him. He was often strict in the way he viewed transgressions of the amateur athletic code, an approach which did not make him universally popular. He also, somewhat unusually, opposed the boycott of Apartheid South Africa. Taking everything into account, however, there is no question that he did much to help the future of the Olympics.

Harold: A Lifetime of Achievement

When he died in 1978, Harold was still dissatisfied that his athletic and other achievements had not been fully recognised in the form of a knighthood[5]. It is a great shame that Chariots of Fire came out after his death, for he would no doubt have taken a

---

[5] In his biography of Harold Abrahams, Mark Ryan speculates whether the activities of Harold's son-in-law, the peace campaigner Pat Pottle, might have had a negative influence. Pat Pottle had helped the double agent George Blake escape from prison and had then been instrumental in providing cover for Blake as he fled the UK for Russia. It seems that Harold never found out about this.

different view about his status and the way in which he was perceived.

For Harold had given so much in his life and his achievements went far beyond his Olympic 100 metres title. At Harold's funeral, Norris McWhirter highlighted Harold's remarkable contribution in ensuring that "track and field athletics today has the status of a national sport." McWhirter also referred to the "near permanence of the IAAF rulebook, which he virtually wrote." In public life, Harold enriched the lives of many and he left a permanent mark on several of the country's great institutions. His private life was also remarkable in the way that he touched the lives of so many in a positive way. As the Duke of Edinburgh put it, Harold was quite simply "one of the most influential figures in the creation and development of athletic competition as we know it today."[6]

---

[6] The Duke of Edinburgh's foreword to Mark Ryan's biography of Harold, "Running with Fire."

CHAPTER 13

The Legend of the Flying Scotsman

"We are all missionaries. Wherever we go, we either bring people nearer to Christ or we repel them from Christ." Eric Liddell

Preparing for China: 1924 – 1925

Sally Magnusson, one of Eric's biographers, once said that "The story in Chariots of Fire stops just before his life got interesting." Having achieved legendary Olympic status, Eric almost immediately left it behind in order to join the London Missionary Service. In doing so, he followed both his father and brother. As Sally Magnuson noted:

"He became this almost celebrity character but was insouciant enough to give that up at a moment's notice. That's what has kept his flame alive. It's what fascinated me."

Even before the Olympics, Eric had begun thinking about his future after Paris. In March 1924, he had applied to the London Missionary Society for work overseas. In this application, he was asked what were his reasons for applying. Eric explained his reasoning as follows:

1. My father worked abroad and that very fact gave an impetus to my designs in that direction.
2. My qualifications in sport give me a natural link with boys at school and college. This gave me an opportunity of using these talents for leading men to the feet of the Master.
3. Being trained as a teacher, I felt that a larger scope was offered for definite Christian work in a college founded on the Word of God, than in a school which was not based on such a foundation.
4. The call of China was so great – China is passing through a critical time, a formative period, which might decide as much for the future of the country, that the very greatness of the work appealed.

After the Olympics, Eric spent a year in Scotland, primarily with D. P. Thomson, in order to hone his skills as a Christian evangelist and to prepare himself more fully for China. In one of his last addresses, at a packed Usher Hall in Edinburgh, he conveyed this message:

"Young, inexperienced, and without eloquence, we have come before you because we feel that we have a message for you… We feel the youth has an appeal to you, and we want to give you our experience. We are placing before you during these few days the thing we have found to be best. We are setting before you one who is worthy of all our devotion, Christ. He is the saviour for the young as well of the old, and he is the one who can bring out what is best in us… Are you living up to the standards of Jesus Christ? We are looking for men and women who are willing to answer the challenge Christ is sending out… Have you sought a leader in everyday life? In Jesus Christ you will find a leader worthy of your devotion and mine. I looked for one I could admire, and I found Christ. I am a debtor, and no wonder I am a debtor, for He has given me a message which can only be experienced. If this audience was out and out for Christ, the whole of Edinburgh would be changed. If the whole of this audience was out and out for Christ, it would go far past Edinburgh and through all Scotland. The last time Edinburgh was swept, all Scotland was flooded. What are you going to do tonight?"

Just days later, following a whirlwind of track races, church services and social engagements, Eric was on his way to China.

The people of Edinburgh lined the route from his old college at Hope Terrace down to Waverley station where he picked up his train. His train carriage had been decorated and huge crowds had gathered to give Eric a send-off befitting the Olympic hero that he was. To cheers and cries of "he's a jolly good fellow!", Eric said a few words:

"I am going out as an ambassador to another country. Our motto should be, "Christ to the world, for the world needs to Christ." I hope that I can be an example of this to the end of my days."

And with that, Eric set off on his way to China where he would join his parents, his sister Jenny, and his brothers Ernest and Rob.

Missionary Life in China: the early years

Eric's journey to China was arduous to put it mildly. He travelled via ferry to Flushing in the Netherlands and by train via Berlin, Riga and Moscow, from where he picked up the Trans-Siberian railway. The Trans-Siberian railway, the longest railway journey in the world, covers a total of 6000 miles and it took Eric seven days to complete it. During his journey, he had plenty of time to read and pray. Amongst the papers he read was his own father's Annual Report of December 1924:

"The past year has seen another civil war, and a change of President, as well as a whole series of changes in personnel of provincial positions, both civil and military. At the same time the country has been brought to a sad condition with regard to railway communications and commerce... The feeling all around is one of suspense, not knowing what will happen next. To those who look on, it seems that no one party is strong enough to command obedience and really govern the country. The government of any one party is flouted by some other although that other may have sworn loyalty to the one in power. It is not surprising that during part of this year Church work has been so difficult. This year we had the triple evils of war, flood and famine. Any one of these is bad enough, but all three together made for something that is very hard to realise. Ruin has overtaken great numbers of families, and it will never be known how many lives have been lost, and may still be lost, through these visitations. Oh, the horror of it all! And to think that so much of it is needless suffering, destruction and waste."

Exactly two weeks after setting off, Eric arrived at Pei – Tai – Ho on the coast of the Bo Hai sea. After spending six weeks with his family there, Eric took the five hour train journey to Tientsin in the west. This is where The Anglo-Chinese College, to which Eric had been assigned, was located and it was soon to reopen in September. In total, Eric spent 12 years teaching at Tientsin with just one year's home leave in 1931–32, during which he was ordained as a minister.

Tientsin had a population of 1½ million at this time and there were many missionaries in the city. The Anglo-Chinese College was for boys, predominantly Chinese, between the ages of 12 and 18. The school had been set up along the lines of a British grammar school and was known as a Middle School in China. All teaching was in English and there were approximately 500 students, generally from good backgrounds. The staff comprised 5 British and 25 Chinese Masters and it was generally seen as one of the better schools in North China.

Eric taught Science and English and, not surprisingly, was also responsible for sport and physical education at the college. Although all the teaching was conducted in English, Eric took it upon himself to learn Mandarin and over the years became quite proficient. Competitive running was also never far away from Eric's life, at least up until 1930. In 1926, he helped design a running track at Tientsin which was modelled on the stadium at Stamford Bridge in London. This track, the Min Yuan Stadium, was at the time considered to be one of the best tracks in Asia and still stands today. Eric himself continued to compete on an occasional basis. For example, in September 1928, Eric defeated a number of Japanese and French Olympic athletes over both 200 metres and 400 metres at a meeting in Manchuria. And in another specially-convened race in 1929, he raced Dr Otto Peltzer, the German world record holder at 880 yards. He beat Peltzer over 400 metres but lost over the longer distance. Eric never ran competitively after 1930.

The college was entirely Christian in its approach and Eric of course took it very seriously. Eric described his bible class work in the following terms:

"I have been taking the Life and Times of Jesus with them. They each have a daily Bible reading card, with instruction as to how to use it with advantage. By this I hope to get them into the habit of (1) Quiet morning prayer; (2) Expectation that the Bible has a message for them which can be applied in their own lives day by day."

Marriage, Family and War

In the summer of 1929, Eric had become romantically involved with a young lady called Florence Mackenzie. Florence was the daughter of missionary parents, Hugh and Agnes Mackenzie, who had returned to Tientsin in 1926. They became formally engaged in May 1930. Eric described the engagement party thus:

"On May 12 there was a large gathering at Mr and Mrs McKenzie's house. There were about 40 people present from the L.M.S. and the United Church of Canada. Just after tea had been served Mr McKenzie announce the engagement of their eldest daughter, Florence – to ME. It was a very happy day indeed. After the announcement we adjourned to the tennis courts where we watched and participated in several sets. Florence and I had to play one of the sets and we fortunately won. I think the other side must have arranged it like that as they thought we ought to win. Florence left for Canada a month later, via England. In Canada she hopes to take a nursing course which will last about three years. After my home leave (1931–2) I hope to return via Canada and if Florence's course is finished we will come out together."

Eric did indeed go on leave in August 1931 and made trips both to Scotland and Canada during this time. In Scotland, he devoted much effort to his evangelistic talks. And it was in Edinburgh on 30 September, at St George's West Church, that he said:

"We are all missionaries. We carry our religion with us, or we allow our religion to carry us. Wherever we go, we either bring people near to Christ, or we repel them from Christ."

Eric returned to Tientsin in the autumn of 1932 and, early in 1934, he and Florence got married. In July 1935 their first daughter, Patricia, was born and, In January 1937, a second daughter Heather was born. It was not until September 1941 that their third daughter, Maureen, was born in Toronto.

In July 1937, war broke out between China and Japan. The Second Sino-Japanese War (July 7, 1937 – September 9, 1945) was a military conflict fought principally between the Republic of

China and the Empire of Japan. It followed the First Sino-Japanese War of 1894–95. China fought Japan with help from Germany, the Soviet Union, the British Empire and the United States. The war later merged into the broader conflict of World War II as a major front of what is known as the Pacific War. The Second Sino-Japanese War was the largest Asian war in the 20th century. It accounted for the majority of casualties in the Pacific War, with somewhere between 10 and 25 million Chinese civilians and over 4 million Chinese and Japanese military personnel dying from war-related causes.

With war now being actively fought, it was obvious that life would get more dangerous very quickly. So it was that Eric, also feeling the call of evangelistic work, decided that he needed to move to the country and a place called Siaochang. Siaochang was some 120 miles inland to the south-west of Tientsin. It was a difficult decision because Florence and the girls could not also be with him on account of the dangerous conditions. But his brother Rob was superintendent of the hospital there so Eric would have some family company. Eric described his first few days:

"So this was Siaochang, the place I would be working at until my home leave (1939 – 40). The first days were spent in language study, for up to then all my work had been in English. We couldn't very easily leave the compound and go into the district owing to the conditions both of the country and of travel, so our thoughts turned to the opportunities at our door. There were many refugees on the compound and it came to us to have a week of meetings mainly for our workers and those living on the premises."

Eric continued to work hard at spreading the Christian word. In the early 1940s, he worked on a book called "The Manual of

Christian Discipleship". This book was later published both in the UK and the USA under the title "The Disciplines of the Christian Life." Eric explained his book as follows:

"In this book I am attempting to do three things:

1. To place before people the limited amount of Christian knowledge that every Christian should have;
2. To help people apply their knowledge to daily life; to live according to the light they have;
3. To develop the devotional life so as to create basic Christian thinking on the subjects of conduct, action, outlook and attitudes.

The Christian life should be a life of growth. I believe the secret of growth is to develop the devotional life.

This involves setting aside each day a time for prayer and Bible study."

During this period Eric certainly had his fair share of danger. Here he describes an event which took place at church:

"I am writing this after an eventful few days. Last Sunday we had planned to hold a big baptismal service for several nearby villages but, already the day before, we heard heavy gunfire in the distance and by breakfast time a scouting plane was circling overhead, so many from the outlying villages didn't turn up, rightly fearing that an attack was about to start. As I addressed those receiving baptism, two shells exploded outside with a terrific noise and there was silence for a moment before we were able to continue. I don't think any who were baptised that day will forget what happened. No one left after the service was over, so we just continued with hymns and witness to keep up our spirits. As there were no opposition forces here, truckloads of Japanese soldiers soon hurtled through the village gates and they searched every building in the place. Though they came into the church they left without causing any real damage, but in the evening, when everyone had gone home and was too frightened to come to the evening service, the church door opened and in came the man who used to be the local opium addict, thanking and praising God. It seems that, having reached a living faith in Christ, he had then been arrested on a trumped-up charge but, unlike many others he had been acquitted. Hurrying home he came to church straight away to give thanks for his deliverance, I'm aware of the terror we had all mine earlier in the day. Feeling I had been given a congregation, I got on with the service!"

Eric's final years

By 1941, life for non-Chinese residents had become extremely difficult and the British government was recommending that all UK citizens should leave the country. In February 1941, the Japanese closed down Siaochang Hospital as well as various foreign residences, thereby effectively closing the Siaochang compound and forcing the missionaries to leave. By 18 February 1941, all the missionaries were back in Tientsin. Shortly afterwards, when Eric and Florence realised that conditions were getting worse in Tientsin itself, they decided that Florence should go back to Canada with their two elder daughters. The fact that Florence was also pregnant with her third child made the decision clear-cut.

In December 1941, Japan bombed Pearl Harbour in the United States. This brought America dramatically into the Second World

War. It also became clear that so-called 'enemy aliens' in Japanese-occupied China were very much at risk. It was surely only a matter of time before such Westerners would be taken captive by the Japanese. In March 1943, this is exactly what happened.

On 12 March 1943, British and American residents, along with other 'enemy nationals' in Tientsin, were instructed to go to the Civil Assembly Centre at Weihsien in Shantung Province. Eric was in the last group to go on 30th March. The internees were permitted to take just four pieces of luggage each, of which one was bedding. Two further suitcases could be carried as hand luggage on the journey. They were then taken by rail from Tientsin some 400 miles to the south east where an internment camp for civil internees had been established. Technically it was not a 'prisoner-of-war' camp as such, although it has been described in such terms.

However described, there is no doubt that life at the camp was extremely brutal and very basic. Typically, four prisoners occupied a room which measured just 9 feet by x 12 feet. The camp had been raided of furniture and other items before the internees arrived. However, a great deal of work was put into the organisation of the camp. A number of "departments" were set up, each with its own team, and there were nine in all:

1. Discipline.
2. Education, Entertainment and Athletics.
3. Employment.
4. Engineering and Repairs.
5. Finance.
6. General Affairs.
7. Medical.

8. Quarters and Accommodation.
9. Supplies.

Eric threw his life and soul into raising the spirits of everyone around him. He set up a school for children in the camp and organised sports such as basketball and rounders fully. He became known as Uncle Eric due to his selfless concerns for his fellow prisoners.

The wife of one of Eric's room mates described Eric's morning routine with her husband as follows:

"Every morning about 6 AM, with curtains tightly drawn to keep in the shining of our peanut oil lamp, lest the prowling sentries should think someone was trying to escape, he used to climb out of his top bunk, past the sleeping forms of his dormitory mates. Then, at the small Chinese table, the two men would sit close together with the light just enough to illumine their bibles and notebooks. Silently they read, prayed, thought about the day's duties, noted what should be done. Eric was a man of prayer not only at set times – though he did not like to miss a Prayer Meeting or Communion service when such could be arranged. He talked to God all the time, naturally, as one can who enters the 'School of Prayer" to learn this way of inner discipline. He seemed to have no weighty mental problems: his life was grounded in God, in faith, and in trust."

By 1945, however, Eric's health was beginning to deteriorate and just six months before the camp was liberated, he died of a brain tumour. It subsequently transpired that Eric had been completely altruistic until the very last. Churchill himself had arranged a passage home which involved a prisoner exchange. But Eric gave up his place to a pregnant woman.

One of his colleagues, Annie Buchan, was with Eric when he died. Annie had been the matron in Siaochang Hospital when Eric and Rob Liddell had been working there and hailed from the Scottish town of Peterhead. After Eric's death, she wrote to DP Thomson:

"I was with him when he died. The last words he said to me were, 'Annie, it is surrender.' He then lapsed into a coma, and about half past nine that evening he went peacefully home."

A fellow survivor of the camp, Langdon Gilkey, said this about Eric:

"Often in an evening I would see him bent over a chess board or a model boat, or directing some sort of square dance – absorbed, weary and interested, pouring all of himself into this effort to capture the imagination of these penned-up youths. He was overflowing with good humour and love for life, and enthusiasm and charm. It is rare indeed that a person has the good fortune to meet a saint but he came as close to it as anyone I have ever known."

One of the most heartfelt tributes to Eric came from a fellow prisoner based on his impressions of life in the camp. On the day of Eric's funeral he wrote as follows:

"He was naturally reserved and tended to live in a world of his own, but he gave of himself unstintedly. His reserve did not prevent him from mixing with everybody and being known by everybody, but he always shrank from revealing his deepest needs and distresses, so that whilst he bore the burdens of many, very few could help bear his.

His fame as an athlete helped him a good deal. He certainly didn't look like a great runner, but the fact that he had been one gave him a self-confidence that men of his type don't often have. He wasn't a great leader, or an inspired thinker, but he knew what he ought to do, and he did it. He was a true disciple of the Master and worthy of the highest of places amongst the Saints gathered in the Church triumphant. We have lost of our best, but we have gained a fragrant memory."

A few days after Eric's death, on Saturday 24th of February, a service was held to commemorate his life. A huge crowd attended. The service was conducted by a senior London Missionary Service missionary, the Reverend Arnold Bryson. Here are some of the words he chose on that day:

"Yesterday a man said to me, "of all the men I have known, Eric Liddell was one in whose character and life the spirit of Jesus Christ was pre-eminently manifested." What was the secret of his consecrated life and far-reaching influence? Absolute surrender to God's will as revealed in Jesus Christ. His was a God-controlled life and he followed his Master and Lord with a devotion that never flagged and with an intensity of purpose that made men see both the reality and power of true religion. With Saint Paul, Eric could say,"I live, yet not I, but Christ liveth in me.""

Eric is buried in the Mausoleum of Martyrs in Siaochang. The city of Weifang, as part of the 60th anniversary of the liberation of the internment camp, marked Eric's life by laying a wreath at his grave in 2005. The memorial had been erected some years before by Edinburgh University. 10 years later, on the 70th anniversary of the liberation of the camp, a statue was erected to commemorate Eric. A ceremony was held to mark the occasion and was attended by Eric's daughters and some of the survivors of the camp. The ceremony was also attended by Joseph Fiennes, the actor playing Eric in an unofficial follow-up version of Chariots of Fire made by a Chinese film crew. The film, entitled, The Last Race, recounts Eric's life in China after the 1924 Olympics.

After all these years, it is remarkable how Eric has lived on in the memory of many Chinese. Eric's daughter Patricia told The Times at the 70th anniversary ceremony that she was taken aback at the statue being erected:

"I find it extraordinary that a statue has been raised – the Chinese don't really raise statues. My father was multi-faceted, he didn't just appeal to religious people. He was born in China, he worked in China, he died in China. He's their Olympic hero. He didn't leave the Chinese people when the going got tough".

The success or otherwise of European missionaries in other parts of the world is often challenged. Some very famous missionaries, such as David Livingstone, achieved very few actual converts to Christianity. But towards the end of the writing of this book, I read that China now has 70 million practising Christians and will soon overtake the United States of America as the country with the single greatest number of Christians. In some part, this must be due to the work of Eric Liddell and his family.

Postscript

CHAPTER 14

Cambridge Revisited

4pm, Sunday 8th November 2013

The Sir Arthur Marshall Room, Cambridge University Athletics Track

I am attending an historic General Meeting of the Achilles Athletics Club. And fittingly, the meeting is being held in the Sir Arthur Marshall room. The Achilles Club was formed in 1920 for past and present members of Cambridge University Athletic Club (CUAC) and Oxford University Athletic Club (OUAC). Achilles is itself a registered athletics club. The club supports CUAC and OUAC both financially and administratively and organises a full programme of domestic competition, overseas tours and domestic and international social gatherings. The club traces its roots back to the first Oxford versus Cambridge Athletic Sports ("Varsity Match") of 1864, an event it still helps to stage each year. OUAC and CUAC members who have competed for their University in the annual Varsity Match are invited to join the Achilles Club.

The specific reason for the meeting is to elect a new President and it turns out that the new President will be only the fourth in its history, despite being founded in 1920. The first President was William Grenfell, the first Baron Desborough, who was an all-round athlete of great distinction as well as being a public servant and politician. Amongst his considerable feats of derring-do, he climbed the Matterhorn three times, swam the Niagara rapids twice and rowed across the English Channel. He was followed by Sir Philip Noel-Baker who was also an outstanding athlete and politician as well as being a diplomat and academic. He was also a renowned campaigner for disarmament. He won an Olympic silver medal at the 1920 Olympics in Antwerp and also received the Nobel Peace Prize in 1959. He remains the only person to have won both an Olympic medal and the Nobel Prize.

The third President was Sir Tommy Macpherson, another all-action hero who, at the time[7], was the most decorated living soldier and who had led a distinguished business career for several decades. Prior to being President, Macpherson had also been Chairman of Achilles. This was a post he had taken over from none other than Harold Abrahams. In 1961, with some club members pressing for change at the top, Macpherson was elected to replace Abrahams. Macpherson went on to make an immense contribution to the club over five decades, organising and raising funds for several overseas athletic tours. Fittingly, on stepping down as President, Macpherson was elected Patron of the club, a post which had only previously been held by Philip Noel-Baker.

The President Elect, Dewi Roberts, is duly voted in as fourth President. The election made, the meeting proceeds to more normal matters and the debate ebbs and flows over donations, spending plans and forthcoming overseas tours. It is reassuring to know that the club remains as focused as ever on ensuring that, ultimately, it is the athletes who benefit from the club and not its officials.

Achilles was founded just four years before Harold Abrahams and Eric Liddell enjoyed their greatest hour at the Paris Olympics. The traditions which were established by the club back then remain undimmed now even as the sport itself, professionalised as it now is, faces threats from doping and drugs abuse on a worrying scale. The club reminds us of a bygone amateur era when sporting values seemed to mean so much more than they

---

[7] Tommy Macpherson died in November 2014 at the age of 94.

do today. As the scandal of widespread doping in athletics reverberates through the sport, we would do well to recall the amateur values of those days.

Eric Liddell and Harold Abrahams did not train as hard as their modern counterparts. But, like all world beaters, they stepped outside of the box. And both were driven by an overwhelming sense of inner purpose – the one derived from subtle discrimination and the other from deep religious conviction. Eric was once asked the secret of his success. He replied: "Why, it's the three sevens!" The "three sevens" refers to the seventh verse of the seventh chapter of the seventh book of the new Testament. That reference is to the first letter of Saint Paul to the Corinthians: "… each one has his own gift from God, one in this manner and another in that." There is no doubt that Eric and Harold both fulfilled their own particular gifts.

Harold Abrahams and Eric Liddell brought distinction to their sport in an era when sporting honour really meant something. Their achievements shall always rank as among the greatest in British athletics. And as men, they shall always rank as among the finest this great sport of athletics has ever produced.

SENIOR OFFICERS OF THE ACHILLES CLUB	
PATRONS	
The Lord Noel-Baker	1979 – 1982
Sir Thomas Macpherson	2013 – 2014
PRESIDENTS	
The Lord Desborough of Taplow	1920 – 1945
The Rt. Hon. P.J. Noel-Baker	1946 – 1979
Sir Thomas Macpherson	1979 – 2013
Dr. D.W. Roberts	2013 –
CHAIRMEN	
The Hon. Montague Shearman	1920 – 1929
P.J. Noel-Baker	1930 – 1936
Bevil Rudd	1937 – 1946
H.M. Abrahams	1947 – 1961
R.T.S. Macpherson	1961 – 1979
Dr. R.K.I. Kennedy	1979 – 1987
H.R.H. Stinson	1987 – 2005
Dr. D.W. Roberts	2005 – 2013
Bridget Wheeler	2013 –

Eric Liddell as a young man

Eric Liddell's signature

Front of Eric Liddell's medals

Back of Eric Liddell's medals

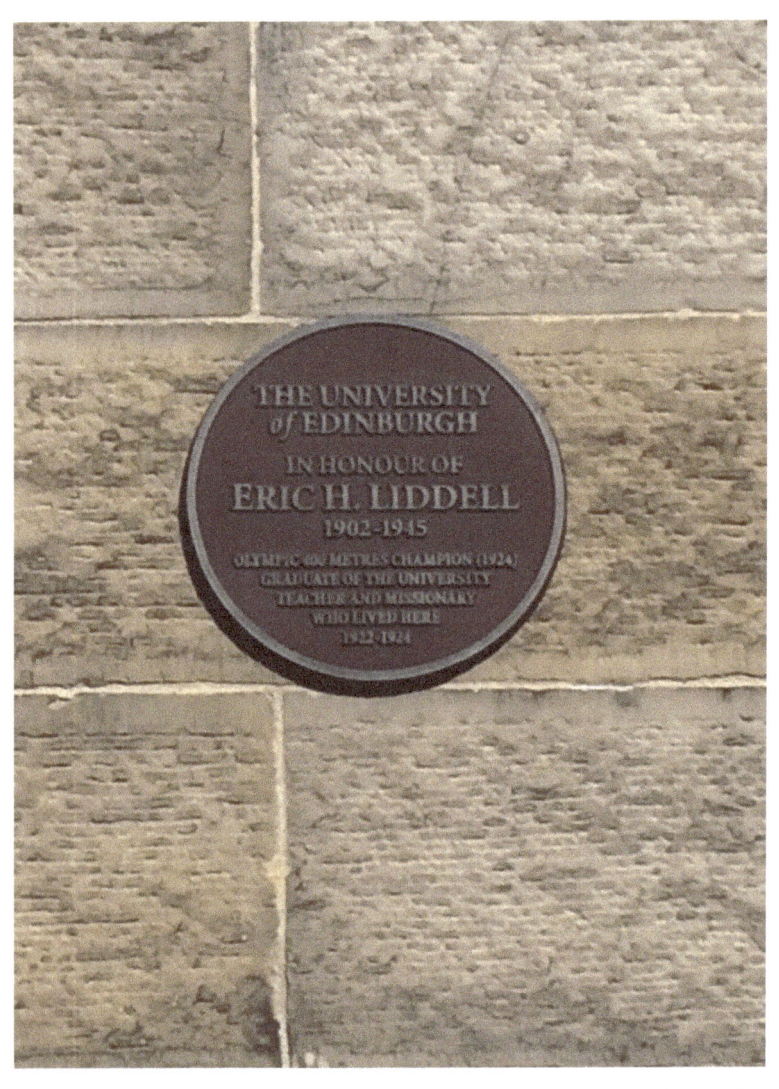

Plaque commemorating Eric Liddell in George Square, Edinburgh

Harold Abrahams takes gold in the 100 yards final

Eric Liddell enjoying tea in his later years

Appendix I

Career Highlights – Harold Abrahams

1918

April
Repton
440 yards – Won (56.6sec)
Long Jump: Won (6.23m/20ft 5½ in)

April 4
100 yards – Won (11.2sec)
220 yards – Won (24.0sec)

April 20
Public Schools Championships at Stamford Bridge, London
100 yards heat – Won (11.0sec)
100yd final – Won (11.0sec)
Long Jump – Won (6.19m/20ft 3¾in)
440 yards – Third

1919
August 29
Aldershot

Race against Willie Applegarth (Abrahams given 2-yard advantage). Won by 6yd (10.0sec)

November 11
Cambridge University Freshman's Sports Day Two
100 yards Final – Won (10.2sec)
Long Jump – Won (6.48 m / 21ft 3in)
440 yards Final – Won (52.8sec)

1920

February 5
Cambridge University's Gonville and Caius College v Oxford University's Magdalene College
100 yards – Won (10.8sec, victory margin 4 yards)
Long Jump – Won (6.36m)
120 yards hurdles – Won (19.2sec, victory margin 3 yards)
440 yards – Won (53.0sec, victory margin 3 yards)

February 24
Cambridge University: Gonville and Caius College v Emmanuel College, (Inter-Collegiate Final)
100 yards – Won (10.2sec, victory margin 2 yards)
Long Jump – Won (6.69m / 21ft 11½ in)
High Jump – Won (1.65m)
120 yards hurdles – Won (18.2sec, victory margin 5 yards)
440 yards – Won (53sec, victory margin 1½ yards)
Caius wins the Rouse Ball Challenge Cup for the first time.

March 12
Cambridge University Sports
100 yards final – Won (10.2sec, narrow victory over Guy Butler)
Long Jump – Won (22 ft or 6.70m)

March 27
Cambridge University v Oxford University at Queen's Club, London
100 yards – Won (10.0sec, victory margin 1 foot over Bevil Rudd)
Long Jump – Won (6.88m or 22ft 7in)

July 10
England v Scotland v Ireland in Crewe
220 yards – Heat: Won (24.2sec, victory margin 6 yards)
220 yards – Final: Won (23.2sec, victory margin 4 yards)
Long Jump: Third (6.49m)

August 15
Antwerp, The Olympic Games
100 metres – Heat 10: Won (11sec)
100 metres – Quarter-final: Fourth and eliminated: (Won by Charley Paddock in 10.8sec)
Long Jump: Third (6.16m)

August 17
Antwerp, The Olympic Games
Long Jump: Twentieth and eliminated before finals (6.05m / 19ft 10¼in)

1921

March 19
Oxford v Cambridge 'Varsity Sports at Queen's Club, London
100 yards – Won (10.2sec –by two feet from Guy Butler)
Long Jump: Third (21ft 4in / 6.51m, compared to winner L.St C. Ingrams' 6.72m)

June 25
London Stamford Bridge
75 yards – Won (7.4sec – This broke the world record by 0.2sec but the track was discovered to be 8 inches too short)

July 2
London Stamford Bridge
The Amateur Athletic Association Championships
100 yards final – Second by half a yard to Harry Edward – who won in 10.2sec (heat and semi final statistics unavailable)
220 yards final – Second by 1½ yards to Harry Edward – who won in 22.2sec.

July 23
Cambridge, Massachusetts
Harvard and Yale versus Oxford and Cambridge
100 yards – Second (won narrowly by Ed Gourdin in 10.2sec)
Long Jump: Second (6.73m. Won by Ed Gourdin with a world record 25ft 3in / 7.69m)

July 28
Travers Island, New York
Oxford and Cambridge versus Princeton and Cornell
100 yards: Won (10.4sec)
Long Jump: Won (6.60m)

November 28
Cambridge University
Inter-Collegiate Championship
100 yards: Won (10.2sec)
Long Jump: Won (23ft / 7.02m)

1922

March 25
Varsity Athletics Match
Oxford University versus Cambridge University
Queen's Club, London
100 yards – Won (10.2 – by one yard from Guy Butler)
Long Jump – Won (6.70m)

1923

March 23
Varsity Athletics Match
Oxford University versus Cambridge University
Queen's Club, London
100 yards – Won (10.0 –the first man to win the Varsity 100 yards four times)
Long Jump – Won (23ft 7¼in / 7.19m –a British record)
440 yards – Won (50.8sec) Beat W.E. Stevenson by 3 yards

July 6
London Stamford Bridge
The Amateur Athletic Association Championships
220 yards – Heat 11: Won (22.4sec)
220 yards – Semi-final: Equal-second with W.P. Nichol (In 22.0sec. Eric Liddell won in 21.6) Abrahams was given chance of a 'run-off' against Nichol for final place. Abrahams declined and withdrew.

July 7
London Stamford Bridge
The Amateur Athletic Association Championships
100 yards – Heat 8: Won (10.2sec) Abrahams withdraws from next round complaining of sore throat.
Long Jump: Won (23ft 8¾in / 7.23m –a new British record)

July 21
Wembley Stadium, London
Oxford and Cambridge v Harvard and Yale
100 yards – Won (10.0sec – margin of victory 3 yards)
Long Jump – Won (23ft 2¼in / 7.07m)
220 yards (straight track) – Won (21.6sec – margin of victory 7 yards)

1924

June 7, Woolwich, London
100 yards final – Won (in a world record-equalling 9.6sec, although Abrahams doubted the validity of the time and concluded there was a slight downward slope on the track)
Long Jump: Won (7.38m)

June 21
The Amateur Athletic Championships
Stamford Bridge, London
100 yards: Final: Won (9.9sec – margin of victory 1 1/2yd over W.P. Nichol)
Long Jump: Won (6.92m)

OLYMPIC GAMES
Colombes Stadium, Paris

July 6
100 metres: Heat 14: Won (11.0sec)
100 metres: Quarter-final 4: Won (10.6sec – equalling the Olympic Record)

July 7
100 metres: Semi-final 2: Won (10.6sec – equalling the Olympic Record again)

100 metres: Final: Won (10.6sec –equalling the Olympic Record for a third time. But on the 1/100th of a second watch he was timed at 10.52sec)

July 8
200 metres: Heat 10: Won (22.2sec)
200 metres: Quarter-final Race 4: Won (22.0sec)

July 9
200 metres: Semi-final 1: Third (21.9sec)
200 metres: Final: Sixth (22.3sec, won by Scholz in 21.6)

July 12
4 × 100 metres relay: Heat 1: Won (42.0sec –a new world record)

July 13
4 × 100 metres relay: Semi-final 2: Won (41.8sec)
4 × 100 metres relay: Final: Second (41.2sec, USA took gold in 41.0 –a new world record) GB Team: H.M. Abrahams, W. Rangeley, L.C. Royle, W.P. Nichol

July 19
London Stamford Bridge
British Empire v USA Relays
4 × 100yd: Second (USA wins by 1 1/2yd in 37.8sec) British Empire Team: A.E. Porritt, E.W. Carr, W.P. Nichol, H.M. Abrahams.
Long Jump: Second (7.07m –won by Ed Gourdin with 7.53m)

July 23
Queen's Club, London
Achilles Club v British Dominions
Long Jump: Second (6.96m –won by S.J.M. Atkinson of South Africa with 7.15m)
100 yards: Third (race won by Arthur Porritt)

August 9
Northampton
All English Championships
Long Jump: Won (7.21m)

1925

April 11
London
Long Jump – First (7.10m)

May 6
London Stamford Bridge: Bedfordshire v London Athletic Club
Long Jump – Second (6.70m –retired injured)

Appendix II

Career Highlights – Eric Liddell

1921

May 28
Edinburgh University Athletic Club Annual Sports, Craiglockhart, Edinburgh
100 yards —1st 10.4
220 yards —2nd
Invitation Relay Race —1st, EUAC, 1: 38.8

June 4
Queen's Park Football Club Annual Sports, Hampden Park, Glasgow
Inter-City Relay Race —2nd, Edinburgh University

June 18
Scottish Inter-Varsity Sports, University Park, St. Andrews
100 yards —1st 10.6
220 yards —1st 22.4

June 25
Scottish Amateur Athletic Association Championships, Celtic Park, Glasgow 100 yards —1st 10.4

220 yards —1st 22.6 (Championship Best Performance)
Mile Relay —1st, EUAC, 3:43.0 (Championship Best Performance)

June 29
Edinburgh Pharmacy Athletic Club Sports, Powderhall Grounds
120 yards (Open) handicap —1st 12.0 off scratch, wind-assisted

July 2
Heart of Midlothian Football Club Annual Sports, Tynecastle Park, Edinburgh 100 yards (Open) handicap —2nd (off scratch)

July 9
Triangular International, Windsor Park, Belfast
100 yards —1st 10.4
220 yards —3rd

July 16
West Kilbride Athletic Club Annual Sports, Seamill Park, West Kilbride
100 yards handicap —1st 10.0 (off scratch)
220 yards handicap —3rd (off scratch)

July 23
Eglinton Harriers Sports, Victoria Park, Salcoats
100 yards handicap —1st 10.0 (off scratch)
220 yards handicap —3rd (off scratch)

July 30
Greenock Glenpark Harriers Meeting, Cappielow Park, Greenock
100 yards Invitational handicap —3rd (off scratch)

August 6
Rangers' Football Club Annual Sports, Ibrox Park, Glasgow
100 yards (Invitation) handicap —1st 10.0 (off 1 yard)
300 yards (Open) handicap —3rd (off scratch)

August 13
Celtic Football Club Annual Sports, Celtic Park, Glasgow
100 yards handicap —1st 10.2 (off 1 yard)
220 yards open handicap —1st 23.6 off scratch)

1922

May 27
Edinburgh University Athletic Club Annual Sports, Craiglockhart
100 yards —1st 10.2 (record)
220 yards —1st 21.8 (record and Scottish native record)
440 yards —1st 52.6

June 3
Queen's Park Football Club Annual Sports, Hampden Park, Glasgow
100 yards (Invitation) handicap —3rd (off scratch)
100 yards (Open) handicap —4th (off scratch)
One Mile Inter-City Relay —2nd Edinburgh 3:46.4

June 17
Scottish Inter-Varsity Sports, King's College, Aberdeen
100 yards —1st 10.4
220 yards —1st 22.8
One Mile Relay Race —1st EUAC, 3:46.8

June 24
A.A.A. Championships, Powderhall Grounds, Edinburgh

100 yards —1st 10.2
220 yards —1st 22.6 (equals Championship Best Performance)
One Mile Relay Race —1st, EUAC, 3:40.0 (Championship Best Performance and Scottish record)

July 8
Triangular International, Hampden Park, Glasgow
100 yards —2nd
220 yards —2nd

July 15
Edinburgh and District Inter-Works Sports, Powderhall Grounds
150 yards (Open handicap) —1st 15.0 (off scratch, equals Scottish native record)

July 26
North British Hotel Annual Athletic Meeting, Powderhall Grounds
100 yards (Open) handicap —1st 10.1 (off scratch)

July 29
Greenock Glenpark Harriers Meeting, Cappielow Park, Greenock
100 yards (Open) handicap —2nd 10.0 (off scratch, equals Scottish native record)

August 5
Rangers Football Club Annual Sports, Ibrox Park, Glasgow
100 yards (Open) handicap, Heat —unplaced
220 yards (Invitation) handicap —1st 22.0 (off 2 yards)

August 12
Celtic Football Club Annual Sports, Celtic Park, Glasgow
120 yards (Invitation) —1st 12.2
220 yards (Invitation) handicap —1st 22.4 (off 2 yards)

1923

May 26
Edinburgh University Athletic Club Sports, Craiglockhart, Edinburgh
100 yards —1st 10.6
220 yards —1st 22.4
440 yards —1st 52.8

June 2
Queens Park Football Club Annual Sports, Hampden Park, Glasgow
100 yards (Invitation) handicap —2nd (off scratch)
Inter-City Relay Race —2nd Edinburgh University 3:40.4

June 16, Scottish Inter-Varsity Sports, Craiglockhart, Edinburgh
100 yards —1st 10.1 (record)
220 yards —1st 21.6 (record)
440 yards —1st 50.2 (Scottish native record)
One Mile Relay —1st EUAC, 3:40.8 (record)

June 23
SAAA Championships, Celtic Park, Glasgow
100 yards —1st 10.4
220 yards —1st 22.4 (Championship Best Performance)
One Mile Relay Race —1st, EUAC, 3:43.6

June 27
Edinburgh Pharmacy A.C. Annual Sports, Powderhall Grounds
120 yards (Open) handicap —1st 11.9 (off scratch)

June 30
Heart of Midlothian Football Club Annual Sports, Tynecastle Park
100 yards (Open) handicap, Heat —1st Semi-final —Unplaced

July 7
A.A.A. Championships, Stamford Bridge, London
100 yards —1st 9.7 (Championship Best Performance and British record)
220 yards —1st 21.6

July 14
Triangular International, Stoke-on-Trent
100 yards —1st 10.4
220 yards —1st 22.6
440 yards —1st 51.2

July 28
Greenock Glenpark Harriers Meeting, Cappielow Park, Greenock
100 yards (Open) handicap, Heat —1st 10.6 (off scratch) Semi-final – Unplaced
100 yards (Invitation) handicap —Unplaced

August 4
Rangers Football Club Annual Sports, Ibrox Park, Glasgow
120 yards (open) handicap, Heat —3rd (off scratch)
300 yards (Special) handicap —4th 31.8 (off scratch)

August 6
British Games Meeting, Stamford Bridge, London
100 yards (Open)Round 1, Heat 1 —1st 10.2
Round 2, Heat 1 —3rd 10.1
Final —4th

August 8
Hibernian Football Club Annual Sports, Easter Road Park, Edinburgh

100 yards (Open) handicap, Heat 3 —1st 10.8 (off scratch) Final —Unplaced
100 yards (Invitation) handicap —Unplaced

August 1
Celtic Football Club Annual Sports, Celtic Park, Glasgow
100 yards (open) handicap —3rd (off scratch)
220 yards (Open) —3rd (off scratch)

1924

April 25–26
University of Pennsylvania Relays, Philadelphia
100 yards (Special Event) —4th
220 yards (Special Event) —2nd

May 19
Maryhill Harriers Meeting, Firhill Park, Glasgow
100 yards Invitation handicap —2nd (off scratch)
Invitation Relay Race —2nd, EUAC 2: 08.8

May 28
Edinburgh University Athletic Club Annual Sports, Craiglockhart
100 yards —1st 10.2 (equals record)
220 yards —1st 23.0
440 yards —1st 51.5 (record)

May 31
Scottish Inter-Varsity Sports, Hampden Park, Glasgow
100 yards —1st 10.2
220 yards —1st 23.4
440 yards —1st 51.2
One Mile Relay Race —1st EUAC, 3:52.8

June 7
Hawick Common Riding Amateur Sports, Volunteer Park, Hawick
100 yards (Open) handicap —2nd (off scratch)
One Mile Relay —1st, EUAC

June 14
SAAA Championships Hampden Park, Glasgow
100 yards —1st 10.0 (equals Championship Best Performance and Scottish native record)
220 yards —1st 22.6
440 yards —1st 51.2

June 20–21
AAA Championships, Stamford Bridge, London
220 yards, Round 1, Heat 1 —1st 22.3 Round 2, Heat 1—1st 21.8
440 yards, Round 1, Heat 3 —1st 51.0 Round 2, Heat 1 —1st 49.6
220 yards Final —2nd
440 yards Final —1st 49.6

June 25
Edinburgh Pharmacy A.C. Annual Sports, Powderhall Grounds
150 yards (Open) handicap, Heat 3 —1st 15.4 (off scratch) Final —2nd

June 28
Heart of Midlothian Football Club Annual Sports, Tynecastle Park
300 yards Invitation handicap —4th (off scratch)

OLYMPIC GAMES
Colombes Stadium, Paris

July 8
200 metres:
Round 1, Heat 3 —1st 22.2
Round 2, Heat 2 —2nd

July 9
200 metres:
Semi-final 2 —2nd 21.8
Final —3rd 21.9 (Bronze Medal)

400 metres:
Round 1, Heat 14 —1st 50.2
Round 2, Heat 4 —2nd 49.3

July 11
400 metres:
Semi-final 2 —1st 48.2
Final —1st 47.6 (Gold Medal, World and Olympic record)

July 19
British Empire v. USA (Relays), Stamford Bridge
London One Mile Relay Race (4 x 440 yards) —1st, British Empire 3:18.2
One Mile Relay (440, 220, 220, 880 yards) —1st, USA 3:29.8, 2nd, British Empire

July 26,
Greenock Glenpark Harriers Meeting (Scotland v. Canada) Cappielow Park
100 yards (International) —3rd
440 yards (International) —1st 51.2
One Mile Relay —1st Scotland 3: 57.0

August 2
Rangers Football Club Annual Sports, Ibrox Park, Glasgow
440 yards Open handicap —1st 49.6 (off scratch)

August 5
West of Scotland Harriers Meeting, Ibrox Park, Glasgow
220 yards Open handicap —3rd (off scratch)
300 yards (off scratch) —1st 32.0

August 16
Gala Harriers Sports, Netherdale Park, Galashiels.
100 yards Open handicap —2nd (off scratch)
440 yards Invitation handicap —1st 54.0 (off scratch)

1925

May 20
Edinburgh University Athletic Club Annual Sports, Craiglockhart, Edinburgh
100 yards —1st 10.4
220 yards —1st 23.0
440 yards —1st 51.4 (record)

May 31
Scottish Inter-Varsity Sports, University Park, St. Andrews
100 yards —1st 10.2
220 yards —1st 22.0
440 yards —1st 55.8

June 6
Queen's Park Football Club Annual Sports, Hampden Park, Glasgow
440 yards (Open) handicap —3rd 50.2 (off scratch)
Inter-City Relay Race —1st Edinburgh 3: 39.8 (Scottish record)

June 13
Corstorphine AAC Sports, Union Park, Corstorphine
440 yards —1st 53.5 (East of Scotland Championship)

June 20
Edinburgh Southern Harriers Annual Sports, Powderhall Grounds
220 yards —1st 23.4 (East of Scotland Championship)
220 yards (Open) handicap —1st 22 1/4 (off scratch)
300 yards Special invitation handicap —1st 31.5 (off scratch)

June 24
Edinburgh Pharmacy A.C. Annual Sports, Powderhall Grounds
120 yards (Open) handicap, heat 5 —2nd (off scratch)
One mile invitation relay —1st, EUAC, 3: 45.4

June 27
SAAA Championships, Hampden Park, Glasgow
100 yards —1st 10.0 (equals Championship Best Performance and Scottish native record)
220 yards —1st 22.2 (Championship Best Performance)
440 yards —1st 49.2 (Championship Best Performance)
One mile relay —1st, EUAC, 3:40.2

Appendix III

Selected writings of Harold Abrahams
The following words are extracts from Harold's book "Athletics" which was published in 1926.

On success in athletics:

Success in athletics, no matter how ambitious or how humble may be the aspirations of the would-be performer, depends essentially on two factors, natural ability and training. It is the combination of these two factors which gives the product, the athlete.

On training techniques:

To prepare for any contest a man must approach it along two connected but different and supplementary routes. First, he has to apply such principles as will enable the body to respond to the strenuous demand when it is made; second, he must so train the body that it acquires the skill needed for the accomplishment of the particular sport which he wishes to practise.

On training for sprinting:

The sprinter will never have to bother his head about tactics or judgement. His only concern is to go hell-for-leather from start to finish. His part is to produce a series of ultra-rapid movements for a very short period. He must train the nervous system to react in a regular manner without even the smallest waste of time, for in a 100 yards race one hundredth of a second represents three and a half inches.

On training for the quarter mile:

Once we leave the realm of pure sprinting and begin to discuss middle distance running, we find that there are two factors which have previously not been present, tactics and judgement.

On training for field events:

Success in field events depends on the training of natural ability so that the athlete can go through a series of complicated and highly specialised movements in a controlled manner.

On the mental side of athletics:

So far we have been almost exclusively concerned in this volume with the discussion on the preparation of the body for athletic performances, but even more important still is the preparation of the mind. A man must train his mind for the contest, he must so adjust his mental outlook to the approaching competition as to secure that everything is working for one end when the time arrives – the achievement of the best performance of which one is capable.

On women in athletics:

The tendency of the 20th century has been towards the total emancipation of women, and as regards athletics there is perhaps more in the use of that word than is habitually supposed. First, let it be said that to condemn the participation of women in track and field athletics as 'preposterous' or 'unwomanly' does not really get us much farther. The general principles laid down in this book are really applicable mutatis mutandis to the other sex.

On the equipment needed for an athletic competition:

Suggested list of paraphernalia for a sports meeting

Two pairs of shorts

Two vests

I suggest two of each because accidents may happen – it may be raining – and, moreover, if you are running in more than one event it is most refreshing to put on a clean attire during the afternoon.

Two pairs of shoes

Here again you may split one pair, and, further, it is advisable to carry about pairs with spikes of different lengths to be used according to the condition of the track.

Jumping or hurdling shoes (when necessary)

Spare pair of laces

Incidentally always test your laces thoroughly before a contest. There is nothing more annoying than to burst a lace as you don your shoes for the start. It is most distressing to yourself and exasperating to the opponents you keep waiting.

Admission ticket and competitor's number (if any)

Money for travelling

Running corks (if you use them) and spare elastic

Tape measure (if you are a long or high jumper) or a thrower of javelins

Pair of trousers

These are to keep warm when you go out to a race, and should be loose so that they can be slipped off at the last minute.

Sweater

Scarf

Overcoat (if the day is bitter)

Toothbrush

It is most refreshing to clean one's teeth before a race and between the heat and the final. The dryness of the mouth on the afternoon of a contest is a usual accompaniment.

Vacuum flask with Tea

This is only necessary if you like hot tea before a race, and if you are going to some outlandish place where there is no means of procuring any.

Slippers

Preferably with crepe soles, and at any rate such as can easily be slipped on and off. No man should walk to the start in spikes and ruin them by marching over all sorts of rough stuff.

Trowel

Toe socks (if you use them)

Appendix IV

Selected writings of Eric Liddell

Paraphrase of 1 Corinthians 13: 4 – 7

Love is very patient, very kind.

Love knows neither envy nor jealousy.

Love is not forward or self-assertive;

love is not boastful or conceited.

It gives itself no airs.

Love is never rude, never selfish, never irritated.

Love never broods over wrongs, love thinks no evil.

Love is never glad when others go wrong.

Love finds no pleasure in injustice,

but rejoices in the truth.

Love is always slow to expose, it knows how to be silent.

Love is always eager to believe the best about a person.

Love is full of hope, full of patient endurance;

love never fails.

Extract from *"Prayers for Daily Use"*

"One word stands out above all others as the key to knowing God, to having his peace and assurance in your heart; it is obedience.

Obedience to God's Will is the secret of spiritual knowledge and insight. It is not willingness to know, but willingness to do (obey) God's Will that brings certainty. "If any man will do (obey) his Will, he shall know of the doctrine, whether it be of God, or, whether I speak of myself." (John 7:17)……

Obedience is the secret of being conscious that God guides you personally.

Every Christian should live a God-guided life. If you are not guided by God you will be guided by something else. The Christian that hasn't the sense of guidance in his life is missing something vital.

To obey God's Will was like food to Jesus, refreshing his mind, body and spirit. "My meat is to do the will of Him that sent me" (John 4:34). We can all have the same experience if we make God's Will the dominant purpose in our lives.

Take obedience with you into your time of prayer and meditation, for you will know as much of God, and only as much of God, as you are willing to put into practice. There is a great deal of truth in the hymn "trust and obey."

When we walk with the Lord,
In the light of His Word,

What a glory He sheds on your way!
While we do his good will,
He abides with us still,
And with all who will trust and obey."

Appendix V

Notes on the film Chariots of Fire

Overview

Chariots of Fire, released in 1981, was produced by David Puttnam, written by the late Colin Welland, and directed by Hugh Hudson. It was nominated for seven Academy Awards and won four, including Best Picture and Best Screenplay. It is ranked 19th in the British Film Institute's list of Top 100 British films. The film is also memorable for the theme tune by Vangelis, who won the Academy Award for Best Original Score. The Chariots of Fire theme tune continues to be used in all manner of sporting events, including the London 2012 Olympics and at the start of what is surely the greatest ultra distance road race in the world, the Comrades marathon in South Africa.

Film Plot

In 1919, Harold Abrahams (played by Ben Cross) goes up to Gonville and Caius College at the University of Cambridge, where he experiences anti-Semitism from the staff. He participates in the Gilbert and Sullivan club and becomes the first person ever to complete the Trinity College Great Court Run – running around the college courtyard in the time it takes for the clock to strike 12. Harold achieves a series of victories in various running competitions. Although focused on his running, he falls in love with a leading Gilbert and Sullivan soprano, Sybil (played by Alice Krige).

Eric Liddell (played by Ian Charleson), born in China of Scottish missionary parents, is first shown competing in a highland games in Scotland. His devout sister Jennie (Cheryl Campbell) disapproves of Eric's plans to compete as an athlete. But Eric sees running as a way of glorifying God before returning to China to work as a missionary.

When they first race against each other, Eric beats Harold. Harold takes it badly, but Sam Mussabini (played by Ian Holm), a professional trainer whom he had approached earlier, takes him on in order to improve his running technique. This attracts criticism from the Masters of the Cambridge colleges (played by John Gielgud and Lindsay Anderson). They claim that it is not gentlemanly for an amateur to employ a professional coach. Harold realises this is a cover for their anti-Semitism and class-based sense of superiority and angrily dismisses their concern.

When Eric accidentally misses a church prayer meeting because of his running, his sister accuses him of no longer caring about God. Eric tells her that though he intends eventually to return to his missionary work in China, he feels divinely inspired when running and that not to run would be to dishonour God. He says that "I believe that God made me for a purpose. But He also made me fast, and when I run, I feel His pleasure."

Both Harold and Eric, after years of training and racing, are accepted to represent Great Britain in the 1924 Olympics in Paris.

Also accepted are Harold's Cambridge friends, Lord Andrew Lindsay (Nigel Havers), Aubrey Montague (Nicholas Farrell), and Henry Stallard (Daniel Gerroll). Just as they are about to board the boat to Paris for the Olympics, Eric learns the news that the heat for his 100 metre race will be on a Sunday. He refuses to run in the 100 metres – despite strong pressure from the Prince of Wales and the British Olympic committee – because his Christian convictions prevent him from running on the Sabbath.

Hope appears in the form of Eric's teammate Lord Andrew Lindsay. Having already won a silver medal in the 400 metres hurdles, Lindsay proposes to give up his place in the 400 metre race on the following Thursday to Eric, who gratefully agrees. His religious convictions supersede national athletic pride and there are newspaper headlines around the world.

Eric delivers a sermon at the Paris Church of Scotland that Sunday, and quotes from Isaiah 40, ending with:

> "But they that wait upon the Lord shall renew their strength; they shall mount up with wings as eagles; they shall run, and not be weary; and they shall walk, and not faint."

Harold is badly beaten by the heavily-favoured United States runners in the 200 metre race. He knows his last chance for a medal will be the 100 metres. He competes in that race and wins. His coach Sam Mussabini is very much overcome with emotion that the years of dedication and training have paid off with an Olympic gold medal. Now Harold can get on with his life and reunite with his girlfriend Sybil, whom he had neglected for the sake of running. Before Eric's race, the American coach remarks dismissively to his runners that Eric has little chance of doing well in the 400 metres due to the length of the race. But one of the American runners, Jackson Scholz, hands Eric a note of support for his convictions. Eric defeats the American favourites and wins the gold medal in a world record time.

The British team returns home triumphant. As the film ends, it is explained that Harold married Sybil, and that he became the elder statesman of British athletics. Eric meanwhile went on to missionary work in China. All of Scotland mourned his death in 1945 in Japanese-occupied China. Eric Liddell was laid to rest, in Weifang, Shandong, along the side of the Yu He River 200 metres from Shengli East Street in China, the country he loved so much.

Historical accuracy of the characters

The film depicts Harold as attending Gonville and Caius College, Cambridge with three other Olympic athletes: Henry Stallard, Aubrey Montague, and Lord Andrew Lindsay. Harold and Stallard were in fact students there and competed in the 1924 Olympics. Montague also competed in the Olympics as depicted, but he attended Oxford, not Cambridge. Aubrey Montague sent daily letters to his mother about his time at Oxford and the Olympics; these letters were the basis of Montague's narration in the film.

The character of Lindsay was based partially on Lord Burghley, a significant figure in the history of British athletics. Although Burghley did attend Cambridge, he was not a contemporary of Harold Abrahams: Harold was an undergraduate from 1919 to 1923 and Burghley was at Cambridge from 1923 to 1927. One scene in the film depicts the Burghley-based "Lindsay" as practising hurdles on his estate with full champagne glasses placed on each hurdle – Burghley did practise in a similar way, but he used matchboxes instead of champagne glasses. The fictional character of Lindsay was created when Douglas Lowe, who was Britain's third athletics gold medallist in the 1924 Olympics, was not willing to be involved with the film.

Another scene in the film recreates the Great Court Run, in which the runners attempt to run around the perimeter of the Great Court at Trinity College, Cambridge in the time it takes the clock to strike 12 at midday. The film shows Harold performing the feat for the first time in history. In fact, Harold never attempted this race, and at the time of filming the only person on record known to have succeeded was Lord Burghley, in 1927. In Chariots of Fire, Lindsay runs the Great Court Run with Harold in order to spur him on and crosses the finishing line just a moment too late. Since the film's release, the Great Court Run has also been successfully run by Trinity undergraduate Sam Dobin, in October 2007.

In the film, Eric is tripped up by a Frenchman in the 400 metres in a Scotland–France international athletics meeting. He recovers, makes up a 20 metre deficit and wins. This was based on fact; the actual race was the 440 yards at a Triangular Contest between Scotland, England and Ireland at Stoke-on-Trent in England in July 1923. His achievement was remarkable as he had already won the 100 and 220 yards events that day. Also not mentioned with regard to Eric is that it was he who introduced Harold to Sam Mussabini. This is indirectly alluded to: in the film, Harold first meets Mussabini while he is watching Eric race. The film, however, suggests that Harold himself sought Mussabini's assistance.

Harold's fiancée is identified incorrectly as Sybil Gordon, a soprano at the D'Oyly Carte Opera Company. In fact, in 1936,

Harold married Sybil Evers, who sang at the D'Oyly Carte but they did not meet until 1934. Also, in the film, Sybil is depicted as singing the role of Yum-Yum in The Mikado, but neither Sybil Gordon nor Sybil Evers ever sang that role with D'Oyly Carte; Evers was known for her charm in singing Peep-Bo, one of the two other "little maids from school". Harold's love of Gilbert and Sullivan, as depicted in the film, is factual.

Eric's sister was several years younger than she was portrayed in the film. Her disapproval of Eric's track career was creative licence; she actually fully supported his athletics. Jenny Liddell Somerville cooperated fully with the making of the film and has a brief cameo in the Paris Church of Scotland during Eric's sermon.

In the film, the 100 metres bronze medallist is a character called Tom Watson; the real medallist was Arthur Porritt of New Zealand, who refused permission for his name to be used in the film, allegedly out of modesty. His wish was accepted by the film's producers, even though his permission was not necessary. However, the brief back-story given for Watson, who is called up to the New Zealand team from the University of Oxford, substantially matches Porritt's history. With the exception of Porritt, all the runners in the 100 metres final are identified correctly when they line up to meet the Prince of Wales.

Jackson Scholz is depicted as handing Eric an inspirational Bible message before the 400 metres final: "It says in the good Book, 'He that honors me, I will honor.' Good luck." In reality, the note was from members of the British team, and was handed to Eric before the race by his attending masseur at the team's Paris hotel. For dramatic purposes, screenwriter Welland asked Scholz if he could be depicted handing the note, and Scholz readily agreed, saying "Yes, great, as long as it makes me look good."

At the memorial service for Harold, which opens the film, Lord Lindsay mentions that he and Aubrey Montague are the only members of the 1924 Olympic team still alive. However, Montague died in 1948, 30 years before Harold's death. As detailed at the start of the book, Sir Arthur Marshall was very much still alive at this time.

Historical accuracy of events in the film

The film takes many liberties with the events at the 1924 Olympics, including the events surrounding Eric's refusal to race on a Sunday. In the film, he does not learn that the 100 metres heat is to be held on a Sunday until he is boarding the boat to Paris. In fact, the schedule was made public several months in advance. Eric did, however, face immense pressure to run on that Sunday and to compete in the 100 metres, being called for a grilling by the British Olympic Committee, the Prince of Wales, and other grandees; and his refusal to run made headlines around the world. The decision to change races was, even so, made well before leaving for Paris and Eric spent the intervening months training for the 400 metres. It is true, nonetheless, that Eric's success in the Olympic 400 metres was largely unexpected.

The film depicts Lindsay, having already won a medal in the 400 metres hurdles, giving up his place in the 400 metres race for Eric. In fact Burghley, on whom Lindsay is loosely based, was eliminated in the heats of the 110 metres hurdles. He went on to win a gold medal in the 400 metres hurdles at the 1928 Olympics but was not entered for the 400 metres.

The film reverses the order of Harold's 100 metres and 200 metres races at the Olympics. In reality, after winning the 100 metres race, Harold ran the 200 metres but finished last, with Jackson Scholz taking the gold medal. In the film, before his triumph in the 100 metres, Harold is shown losing the 200 metres and being scolded by Mussabini. And during the following scene in which Harold speaks with his friend Montague while receiving a massage from Mussabini, there is a French newspaper clipping showing Scholz and Charlie Paddock with a headline which states that the 200 metres was a triumph for the United States. In the same conversation, Harold laments getting "beaten out of sight" in the 200 metres. The film thus has Harold overcoming the disappointment of losing the 200 metres by going on to win the 100 metres, a reversal of the real order.

In the film the Canadian Flag is shown with a maple leaf; however, in the 1920s it was either the Red Ensign or the Union Jack. The Maple Leaf only became the national flag in 1965.

Eric also ran in the 200 metres race and finished third behind Paddock and Scholz. This was the second time that Eric and Harold competed in the same race.

Harold also won a silver medal as an opening runner for the 4 x 100 metres relay team, which is not shown in the film. Aubrey Montague placed sixth in the steeplechase, as depicted.

Historical accuracy of the filming locations

The beach scenes associated with the theme tune were filmed at West Sands, St. Andrews. A plaque commemorating the filming can be found there today. The very last scene of the opening titles crosses the 1st and 18th holes of the Old Course at St. Andrews

Links. In real life, athletes from the 1924 team trained and spent time in Broadstairs, Kent, as depicted in the film.

As they run off the beach towards their hotel, the athletes are shown staying at a hotel called The Carlton. The real hotel – as used by the 1924 Olympic athletes – is now a care home in Broadstairs.[8]

All of the Cambridge scenes were actually filmed at Hugh Hudson's old school Eton College, because Cambridge refused filming rights, fearing depictions of anti-Semitism. The Cambridge administration regretted the decision after the film's enormous success.

Liverpool Town Hall was the setting for the scenes depicting the British Embassy in Paris. The Colombes Olympic Stadium in Paris was represented by The Oval Sports Centre, Bebington, Merseyside. The nearby Woodside ferry terminal was used to represent the embarkation scenes set in Dover. The railway station scenes were filmed at the National Railway Museum in York. The scene depicting a performance of The Mikado was filmed in the Savoy Theatre with members of the D'Oyly Carte Opera Company. The dinner scene between Harold and Sybil was filmed at the Café Royal Oyster Bar in Edinburgh.

---

[8] I am indebted to fellow writer Mike Fleet for this information.

Appendix VI

Recollections of Eric Liddell By Sir Arthur Marshall

The Cambridge University Athletics Club had an invitation from Pennsylvania to take a team of seven to the Pennsylvanian Games in March 1924, and I was one of the seven. Eric Liddell, the Scot from Edinburgh University, the 1923 AAA 100 yards Champion, had been personally invited and travelled with us. We stayed at the very comfortable Pennsylvanian Cricket Club. I am afraid none of us, including Eric Liddell, managed to win an event at the Pennsylvanian Games.

We travelled back in a small slow ship of the American United Line called 'The Republic' – a ten day crossing. Eric Liddell entered in the fun and games on the boat, including the Fancy Dress Dance. Whilst he was very strict about religion, Eric and I became good friends and saw much of two American sisters, Freddie and Edith, who were travelling to 'do Europe', including the UK. They said they were going to be in Paris for the Olympic Games, and we said if we were there at the same time we hoped we could meet.

Harold Abrahams had set his whole life on winning the Olympic 100 Metres – it had become an obsession with him. Liddell's achievement in winning the 1923 AAA 100 Yards in the record time of 9 7/10 seconds was a devastating blow to Abrahams and shook him to the core. To date Abrahams had been a consistent 10 seconds 100 yards winner but had only slightly broken 10 seconds on one or two occasions. He knew in the Olympics he would be up against overseas competition, particularly from the Americans, but this new and very serious opposition out of the blue and on his doorstep had come at a time when Harold had established his 100 yards supremacy in the UK. To achieve level pegging with Eric Liddell's new record time, Harold had to improve his performance by two or three yards with the help of his trainer Sam Mussabini. It must have been a tremendous relief to Harold when it became known early in 1924 that Eric had decided to concentrate on the 400 metres and, because of his religious principles, would not compete in the Olympic 100 metres as first heats were always run on Sunday.

Eric had in turn become completely dedicated to winning an Olympic Medal within the restrictions of his faith. He was a famous Scottish international rugger player, and gave up his rugger to enable him to concentrate on his Olympic ambitions, which became very deep-rooted, and his work suffered. Winning an Olympic Gold Medal became a priority, second only to his religion, and the ambition to win this event became part of his religion.

The team travelled to Paris days before the Olympics started and had a big send-off at Victoria Station.

The silence at the start of the 100 metres and 400 metres was quite electric. Harold Abrahams won the 100 metres in a new Games record time.

In spite of all that has been said about Abrahams' 100 metres, the 400 metres in some way provided the greatest thrill of the meeting with the world record being broken by Eric Liddell three times in two days. It was thought that Liddell had some chance of winning, but nobody thought Liddell capable of the amazing performance he achieved in the final. As far as the crowd were concerned they were well informed about Liddell's dedication to his religion and his refusal to run in the first round of the 100 metres on the Sunday; they also knew of his determination to win this event. The occasion was enlivened by the support given to Liddell by the pipes and drums of the Cameron Highlanders.

The silence and pent-up excitement at the start of the race could be felt. Liddell went ahead at the start and maintained his pace throughout, finishing in what at the time was described as 'a most lion-hearted manner' winning by three yards from Fitch, an American. This was probably the greatest achievement of the VIIIth Olympiad, and superlatives were showered on Liddell by the press of the entire world. Liddell was short and not a pretty runner but just pounded along virtually at the same pace all the way, with a finish as if he was making a final dash for a try in a rugger match with an opponent bearing down on him and about to tackle from behind.

After Eric had won the 400 metres Gold Medal, Eric and I made contact with Freddie and Edith, the American sisters, and took them to a Tango Tea Dance in the Champs Elysees.

Appendix VII

Obituary, 17 March 2007: Sir Arthur Marshall

Reproduced by kind permission of The Telegraph Media Group Limited

© *Telegraph Media Group Limited 2007/2015*

Sir Arthur Marshall, who died yesterday aged 103, was a towering figure in British aviation, having developed a modest 1920s car hire and garage business into Marshall of Cambridge, the internationally renowned aerospace engineering company.

Combining his entrepreneurial flair and his engineering and flying skills with his father's belief that, after the First World War, there would be a sound future for aviation, Marshall placed the company in pole position to profit from rearmament and wartime contracts in the 1930s and 1940s.

At the same time he devised a revolutionary procedure for the rapid training of pilots and their flying instructors; during the Second World War the Marshall Flying Schools trained more than 20,000 pilots and instructors for the RAF, and its methods continue to be used by the RAF to this day.

The 1939–45 war also saw the beginnings of Marshall's aircraft repair organisation. During the conflict the company repaired more than 5,000 aircraft, Marshall often test-flying the repaired aircraft himself. After the war he built huge servicing hangars at Cambridge and constructed a runway capable of accepting the largest aircraft – the only such runway in Britain built without public funding.

Recession did not inhibit the steady growth of Marshall's company. Among many initiatives, he contracted to design and build Concorde's distinctive droop nose and he established at Cambridge a thriving technical centre for the RAF's Hercules and TriStar fleets.

In support of his aviation activities Marshall established a commercial vehicle and bus-building facility with a peak production of 140 a week. At one time he supplied more than 80 per cent of Britain's military thin-skinned vehicles and buses.

Meanwhile he further expanded the company's garage group to 20 depots throughout the south-east, selling a wide range of cars and commercial vehicles. Remarkably, every Marshall initiative – including the provision of an airport for Cambridge at no cost to the community – was self-financed.

The eldest of eight children, Arthur Gregory George Marshall was born on December 4 1903 at Cambridge. His father, David, had begun as a 14-year-old kitchen boy at Trinity College before becoming steward of the Pitt Club and going on to start a car hire service with two chauffeur-driven limousines.

Arthur was six when his father launched the Brunswick Motor Car Company in a former stable. In 1914, however, fearing that

Brunswick sounded too German, David Marshall renamed the business Marshall's Garage. During the First World War he also organised Army and munitions factory canteens.

When the war ended Arthur's early interest in aviation was further stimulated when his father returned home with a surplus Handley-Page bomber, which he had picked up for a fiver and installed in the grounds of his Cambridge home, which he re-named Aviation Hall.

In 1919 Arthur and his father were taken up for their first flight (the fare was 10 shillings each). After circling Brighton pier in a Fairey 111A seaplane they were convinced where the firm's future lay.

But first Marshall senior had to restore the garage business, neglected during the war years, while his son progressed from Tonbridge School to Jesus College, Cambridge, where he shone as an athletics Blue (he was selected as a reserve for the British team for the 1,600 metres at the Paris Olympics in 1924).

After graduating with a First in Engineering, Arthur Marshall joined the family business in 1926 and qualified as a pilot at the Norwich and Norfolk Flying Club. Shortly afterwards he bought a de Havilland Gipsy Moth for £740, housing it at home in a paddock hangar opening on to a private landing ground at Fen Ditton.

He began to fly his father to race meetings, to obtain orders for aeroplanes and to teach the purchasers to fly. In October 1929 the landing ground became the company's first aerodrome and the base of its flying training school. Marshall was to be made a master instructor by the Guild of Air Pilots in 1931 after completing only 70 hours, and his pupils would include the future test pilots Bill Humble and HG Barrington.

In 1930 Marshall met Rosemary Dimsdale, a bluestocking granddaughter of the 6th Lord Dimsdale. He taught her to fly, and after they married in 1931 they toured Switzerland and Italy on a flying honeymoon in Marshall's Puss Moth.

In 1932 they flew to the south of France on the first of a series of annual holidays which lasted until the eve of war. The garage business began to make shell covers, converted Austin 12s into armoured cars and equipped Tiger Moth trainers with bomb racks to be used in the event of an invasion. Once the threat of invasion had receded Marshall concentrated on the company's two flying schools; before long Marshall of Cambridge accommodated the largest of the Elementary Flying Training Schools.

Meanwhile, Marshall's Aircraft Repair Organisation grew until it was handling a wide range of military aircraft, including Flying Fortresses, Mosquitoes, Typhoons and Hamilcar gliders as well as battle-weary Spitfires and Hurricanes.

Although he became chairman and joint managing director in 1942, Marshall kept his hand in as an instructor and continued to fly, despite increased executive burdens following his father's death in that year.

The immediate postwar problem was to restore the company's pre-war, bread-and-butter motor business, and this preoccupied Marshall until 1948, when the Berlin Airlift required the rapid servicing of a variety of RAF aircraft. Thereafter, as the RAF re-equipped with jets, the aircraft engineering floodgates opened.

Marshall collected contracts throughout the aircraft industry, and from the 1950s his workshops were busy with Venoms, Vampires, Canberras, Valiants and the civil Viscount. At the same time his Cambridge aerodrome was a centre for flying training, including that of the Cambridge University Air Squadron.

In the 1960s, amid government pressures to rationalise the aircraft industry and the cancellation of the TSR2 advanced swing-wing aircraft (in which project the company was involved), Marshall kept the business afloat.

And then came his great break. Hearing of RAF interest in Lockheed's Hercules C-130 transport aircraft, he was contracted to open a Hercules technical centre. From 1964 Marshalls provided design, repair and modification facilities for the world's celebrated air transport workhorse and other Lockheed products.

In the early 1970s Marshall diversified into space artefacts and specialised containers to hold sophisticated equipment, including black boxes; always keen to encourage youth training, he supported Air Training Corps adventure schemes. Marshall himself remained youthful and adventurous, and in 1978, at the age of 75, he upgraded his pilot's licence so that he was licensed to fly the company's new Citation 2 communications aircraft.

In September 1980 the Ministry of Defence placed a moratorium on all defence contracts. A saddened Marshall ordered redundancies; then, in 1982, he had to expand once again to meet the needs of the Falklands campaign.

Winning a contract to provide the Hercules with air-to-air refuelling, he put a rejuvenated design office to work. Contracts were again falling off when TriStar transport-tanker conversions saved the day, and Marshall rapidly expanded the design office.

In 1989 he handed over the reins as chairman and chief executive to his elder son, Michael, accepting that, at 83, it was time to step aside; to the end he had continued to work seven days a week. Saying goodbye, Marshall thanked his sisters Margery and Violet for their services as directors and wished Michael and his colleagues "the best of Marshall luck". In 1994 he published The Marshall Story – a century of wheels and wings.

Arthur Marshall was appointed OBE in 1948 and knighted in 1974. In 1990 he was awarded the Order of El Istiqual First Class by King Hussein of Jordan. He was commissioned a Deputy Lieutenant for Cambridgeshire in 1968 and served as High Sheriff for Cambridgeshire and the Isle of Ely in 1969–70. He was elected Companion of the Royal Aeronautical Society in 1980 and an honorary fellow of Jesus College, Cambridge, in 1990.

With his wife Rosemary, who died in 1988, he had two sons and a daughter.

Appendix VIII

Bring Me My Chariot of Fire

The title "Bring Me My Chariot of Fire" is taken from the hymn "Jerusalem". It was this hymn which inspired the title of the film "Chariots of Fire" and which is heard in the closing sequences as the characters run along the beach. The hymn started life as a poem by William Blake and appears in the preface to his work "Milton: a Poem" (1804). It subsequently re-surfaced in 1916 when it was included in a patriotic anthology of verse. This was a time when morale was low due to the high number of casualties in the First World War. Because the poem seemed to define what Britain was fighting for, C. Hubert H. Parry was asked to put it to music. Considered to be England's most popular patriotic song, it is sometimes used as an alternative national anthem.

The poem was inspired by the story that a young Jesus, accompanied by Joseph of Arimathea, visited Glastonbury in England during his unknown years. The poem is linked to the Book of Revelation which describes a Second Coming in which Jesus establishes a New Jerusalem. Jerusalem is considered to be a metaphor for heaven in the Christian Church. The poem is commonly interpreted to mean that Jesus would briefly create heaven in England, by contrast to the "dark Satanic Mills" of the Industrial Revolution.

BRING ME MY CHARIOT OF FIRE

The line "Bring me my Chariot of fire!" comes from the Book of Kings in the Old Testament in which the prophet Elijah is taken to heaven:

"And it came to pass, as they still went on, and talked, that, behold, there appeared a chariot of fire, and horses of fire, and parted them both asunder; and Elijah went up by a whirlwind into heaven."

The phrase is thus synonymous with divine energy.

Jerusalem

And did those feet in ancient time
Walk upon England's mountains green?
And was the holy Lamb of God
On England's pleasant pastures seen?

And did the Countenance Divine
Shine forth upon our clouded hills?
And was Jerusalem builded here
Among those dark Satanic Mills?

Bring me my Bow of burning gold;
Bring me my Arrows of Desire;
Bring me my Spear; O clouds unfold!
Bring me my Chariot of Fire!

I will not cease from Mental Fight,
Nor shall my Sword sleep in my hand,
Till we have built Jerusalem
In England's green and pleasant Land.

Appendix IX

Correspondence with Brian Boulton, former pupil of Eltham College

From: Hugh Shields

To: Members of the NUTS Historical Group November 2015

I thought to let you know that I have nearly finished my book which tells the true story of Chariots of Fire. My plan is to publish it so as to coincide with a film on Eric Liddell due out next spring/early summer. It is provisionally titled "Bring me my Chariot of Fire".

If anyone has interesting snippets or suggestions on this subject, I will happily receive them; although I have nearly finished the first draft, I will re-work it quite a bit before finalising it.

I hope to make the next meeting, work travels permitting.

Best wishes

Hugh

Author of "Showdown in Moscow"

From: Brian Boulton

To: Hugh Shields

Dear Hugh,

With regard to your book, provisionally entitled "Bring me my Chariot of Fire", I am interested in this as I was at Eltham College from 1952 -1959 . As you will probably know there were two houses used by boarders situated in Grove Park Road in addition to the main accommodation for boarders housed in the school premises. One of these properties was called "Liddell House". No doubt you also have seen a copy of the booklet entitled "Eric Liddell – The Making Of An Athlete And The Training Of A Missionary" by D. P. Thompson printed by the Eric Liddell Memorial Committee, I believe in the early 1950's. To my knowledge there have also been two books published regarding the history of the school containing references to "Liddell" i.e. "The Glory of The Sons" 1952 and Eltham College Past and Present (a re-print) with updating 1950 -1990 published in 1992.

I was Athletics Captain at "Eltham" in my final year, when Bob Carter was given a time of 10.1 seconds when winning the 100 yards championship on Sports Day when the existing record at the time was 10.2 seconds, I believe attributed to Liddell. In my draft report that summer as Athletics Captain I made no mention of this "record" and was asked to explain. My response was that I did not consider it a valid performance as the 100 yards run on a downhill course, was also extremely wind assisted, and Bob Carter had never previously run anywhere near that time. As a consequence, I was later given to understand that arguments over the matter went on for a number of years! In due course the distances went metric which stopped any further argument and also wiped out my school 880 yards and 1 mile records.

Brian

From: Hugh Shields

To: Brian Boulton

Dear Brian, thank you very much for taking the time to write back with such an interesting personal story. I am indeed familiar with the DP Thompson work but not the other books to which you refer.

I touch on Liddell's time at Eltham College and would love to include your story if you are happy for me to do so. It would sit very well in the short chapter I have on his early years. 10.2 for 100 yards as a schoolboy – impressive stuff alright.

I was at boarding school in Scotland when I first heard about Eric Liddell and it was a little bit before Chariots of Fire was released. With his rugby pedigree as well, he instantly acquired hero status to me.

Thank you again for writing and please do let me know if you would allow me to refer to your story in my book.

Regards, Hugh

From: Brian Boulton

To: Hugh Shields

Dear Hugh,

Thanks for your reply.

I am happy for you to use whatever you wish from what I have written. For some years now I have been making regular donations to the school's annual fund. As a result of which I am invited back each summer as a token of thanks, and get to view the progress and changes that have taken place in the foregoing 12 months. I am thus known to some of the current staff.

In addition, I believe I have some photographs taken by my father of the 1959 Eltham College sports day at least one of which shows a huddle of physics and maths department staff around the finish line. From my own experiences as a timekeeper I would not like to guarantee the accuracy of their times in that situation. There may also be some old sports day programmes in my parents papers, but at the moment I am not sure where to look for them.

Regards

Brian

Appendix X

Article from The Daily Telegraph, August 2015

Chariots of Fire champion hailed as a national hero in China

Reproduced by kind permission of The Telegraph Media Group Limited

© *Telegraph Media Group Limited 2007/2015*

By Isabelle Fraser 18 Aug 2015

A British Olympic hero whose story was illustrated in the film Chariots of Fire has been named by a Chinese city as a national hero.

Eric Liddell, who was nicknamed The Flying Scotsman, famously won a gold medal at the 1924 Olympic Games in Paris.

He had been due to take part in the 100m but could not because his strong Christian faith prohibited him from running in the heats which fell on a Sunday. He had to choose between his sport and religious beliefs – and retrained to win the 400m.

Imprisoned in an internment camp by the Japanese in World War Two, Liddell is viewed by many Chinese as a hero for his sporting prowess and acts of benevolence while in a Japanese prisoner-of-war camp.

Liddell was born in Tianjin, the city in north-eastern China which was recently hit with massive explosions.

He was educated in Britain, but returned to China as missionary. He chose to stay on and continue his work even after Japan's invasion of China in 1941, despite having the opportunity to flee.

He was interned at a camp in Weifang, south of Tianjin – and it is here that a statue of Liddell has been unveiled.

The camp was liberated 70 years ago, and as the statue was revealed, some survivors of the camp were present, as were his daughters.

Joseph Fiennes was also present, who is starring in an unofficial sequel to Chariots of Fire, called The Last Race, which has been filmed in China and co-written by a Hong Kong director.

Winston Churchill had organised for Liddell's release from the internment camp, but he instead gave his ticket to a pregnant woman who was also in the camp.

He also smuggled medical supplies through barbed wire and helped to educate internees. His family fled the country in 1941 for Canada.

Liddell died in the camp in February 1945 of a brain tumour.

Liddell's family say that his strength and benevolence were forged by his Christianity – and his decision to stay even after the invasion by Japan made him into a cult figure in China.

Patricia Liddell, 80, told The Times: "I find it extraordinary that a statue has been raised – the Chinese don't really raise statues, maybe just for Mao Zedong."

She added: "My father was multi-faceted, he didn't just appeal to religious people. He was born in China, he worked in China, he died in China. He's their Olympic hero."

Mr Fiennes said: "It's not just preaching, it's about watching someone in a set of beliefs in extraordinary circumstances still believing those beliefs will carry him through."

Lightning Source UK Ltd.
Milton Keynes UK
UKHW052008150322
400098UK00003B/211/J